PRE-K · MATH · AGES 4–5

by Nathalie Le Du

illustrated by Les McClaine

educational consulting by Randi House

Odd Dot · New York

LET'S LEARN ABOUT

Same & Different

Circle the plants that are the **same** in each row.

What makes these plants the same? Talk about your ideas with a friend or family member.

Cross out the plant that is **different** in each row.

1
Same & Different

When you match objects, the objects look the same and the names also sound the same. Find matching objects around you and say their names aloud!

TinkerActive Pre-K Math Workbook 3

Read the name of each color aloud. Then draw a line from each color to the matching paint tube, and say the name again.

Red

Orange

Yellow

Green

Blue

Look at each creature and say its color. Then color the creature next to it a **different** color. Last, say the name of the different color aloud.

1
Same & Different

TinkerActive Pre-K Math Workbook 5

The MotMots are spreading seeds. Draw a line along the same path where the group spread seeds.

Callie, Amelia, and Brian are playing follow-the-leader, and they have to copy each other's movements. Cross out the MotMot that is doing something **different** in each row.

1
Same & Different

Play follow-the-leader with your friends! Choose the leader and copy all the moves until someone makes a mistake. Take turns being the leader.

7

LET'S START!   GATHER THESE TOOLS AND MATERIALS.

White paper

Red, yellow, and blue crayons

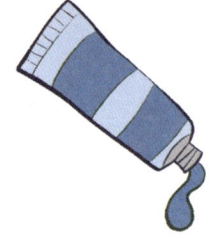
Washable paint

Paint brush

Construction paper

Glue or tape

Scissors
(with an adult's help)

LET'S TINKER!

Lay a piece of white paper in front of you. **Color** an area with your red crayon. Next, **color** on top of the same area with a yellow crayon. What color do you get? **Combine** your crayon colors to make different colors.

LET'S MAKE: MIRROR IMAGE BUTTERFLY!

1. Fold a piece of paper in half. Then **open** it up so it lies flat.

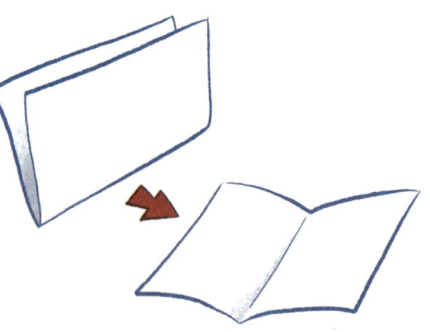

2. Paint half the body of a butterfly on one side of the paper.

3. Paint one wing of the butterfly on the same side.

4. Carefully **fold** your paper again, pressing the paint onto the other side.

1

Same & Different

5. Open the paper and paint antennae and eyes. Then let it dry.

Are the wings of the butterfly the same or different? Why?

LET'S ENGINEER!

Oh no! The squirrels got into Frank's flower patch and ate all the tulips.

How can the MotMots replace Frank's tulips to cheer him up?

Make or build tulips for Frank using your materials. **Do** your best to make them look just like the tulips in Frank's garden. When you are done, **compare** them to the picture. How are they the same? How are they different?

PROJECT 1: DONE!
Get your sticker!

LET'S LEARN ABOUT Matching & Making Sets

Shape is the form of an object. For example, wheels have a round shape. Circle the blocks that are the **same shape** in each row.

Size is how big an object is. For example, an ant is small and a car is large. Cross out the blocks that are **small** in each row.

2
Matching & Making Sets

Circle the blocks that are **large** in each row.

Follow the directions to sort the objects two ways.

Cross out the toys that are **red**.
Then circle the toys that are the **same shape**.

Cross out the toys that are **blue**.
Then circle the toys that are the **same shape**.

Cross out the toys that are **yellow**.
Then circle the toys that are the **same shape**.

2

Matching & Making Sets

Cross out the toys that are **orange**.
Then circle the toys that are **large**.

Cross out the toys that are **green**.
Then circle the toys that are **small**.

Cross out the toys that are **purple**.
Then circle the toys that are **large**.

After sorting, say these sentences aloud and fill in the missing words: Some of these toys are the color _____. And some of these toys are the same size.

It's time to clean up! Draw a line from each toy to the correct bin.

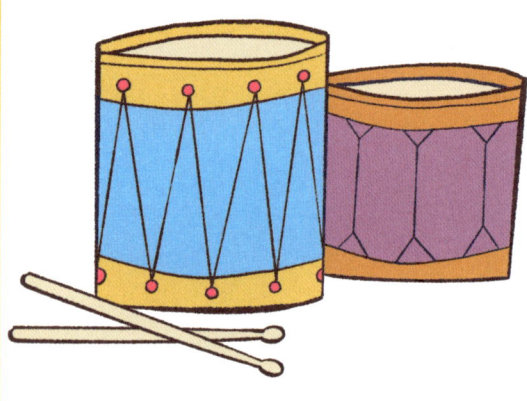

2

Matching & Making Sets

LET'S START!

GATHER THESE TOOLS AND MATERIALS.

Different colored blocks or small toys

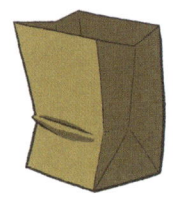
Paper bags

Crayons or markers

Construction paper

Scissors (with an adult's help)

Glue or tape

LET'S TINKER!

Sort your materials two or more times: **Gather** your blocks or toys in a paper bag and shake them up. **Pull** out one item at a time, and sort each toy by its color. Now, **put** everything back in and sort the toys by their shapes. **Put** everything back in again and sort by their sizes. Are there any other ways you can sort the objects? **Make up** your own categories, like things that roll or stand.

LET'S MAKE: MATCHING MONSTERS!

1. Choose a few different colors of construction paper.

2. With the help of an adult, **cut** monster face shapes out of the paper, including a hole for the mouth. (The hole should be large enough to put a block or toy through it.)

3. **Glue** or tape each monster's face to the front of a paper bag.

4. With the help of an adult, **cut** a hole in the bag where the mouth goes.

2
Matching & Making Sets

5. **Decorate** each monster as you like.

6. **Open** the bags and stand them up on a flat surface. Fold over the top of each bag.

7. **Feed** the hungry monsters! **Pile up** your blocks or toys in front of your monsters. **Feed** each monster the color it likes to eat! Blue monsters like blue toys, red monsters like red toys, and so on.

LET'S ENGINEER!

The MotMots want to play dress-up, but the costume closet is a mess!

How can the MotMots sort the closet so everyone has a complete costume?

With the help of an adult, **look** in a closet or some drawers. Can you match a whole outfit for yourself from head to toe? **Explain** why the clothes belong together. Is it a costume or an outfit you can wear every day?

PROJECT 2: DONE!
Get your sticker!

LET'S LEARN ABOUT Counting to 10

Follow the path from 1 to 5 with your finger and say each number aloud. Then draw a line from 1 to 5 to complete the picture.

Count how many fingers each MotMot is holding up. Then trace the number.

3

Counting to 10

Follow the path from 0 to 10 with your finger and say each number aloud. Then draw a line from 0 to 10 to complete the picture.

Count how many fingers each MotMot is holding up. Then trace the number.

Counting to 10

The MotMots are playing Enid Says Count Aloud! Play along with them by following each direction and counting aloud.

 **Enid Says:** Touch your nose **5** times.

 **Enid Says:** Touch your toes **3** times.

 **Enid Says:** Jump **8** times.

 **Enid Says:** Stomp your feet **10** times.

Play your own game of Enid Says Count Aloud! Get some friends and choose a leader. The leader says what the other players must do and how many times they must do it. But only follow commands that begin with the words "Enid Says." Listen carefully! If you do an action without the leader saying "Enid Says," you're out!

Look at the key, and color the MotMots by matching each number to a color.

3

Counting to 10

0 = **red**
1 = **orange**
2 = **yellow**
3 = **green**
4 = **yellow-green**
5 = **blue**
6 = **brown**
7 = **purple**
8 = **teal**
9 = **pink**
10 = **black**

LET'S START!

GATHER THESE TOOLS AND MATERIALS.

10 paper cups

Crayons

55 small snacks, like: cereal, nuts, raisins, mini pretzels, etc.

Markers

Pencil

White paper

Scissors (with an adult's help)

Craft sticks

Glue or tape

Empty egg carton

LET'S TINKER!

Put 10 paper cups in front of you. With the help of an adult, **write** a number from 1 to 10 on each cup. **Mix up** your cups. Can you put them back in order from 1 to 10? How about from 10 to 1? Can you fill each cup with the correct number of snacks? When you are done, **open** your own snack stand and sell your snacks!

LET'S MAKE: COUNTING PUZZLE!

1. **Create** a drawing on a horizontal piece of paper using your crayons.

2. With the help of an adult, **draw** 10 straight lines from top to bottom using a pencil.

3. Number each section of your drawing from 0 to 10 using a pencil.

4. With the help of an adult, **cut** the drawing along each line.

3

Counting to 10

5. Mix up the pieces of paper so they are out of order.

6. Reveal your picture again by putting the numbered pieces of paper in order!

LET'S ENGINEER!

The night before Tinker Town's street fair, a windstorm hit the town and blew away all the street signs! No one will be able to find their way from the beginning of the street fair at 1st Street to the end at 10th Street.

How can the MotMots help everyone know which is 1st Street, 2nd Street, 3rd Street, and so on?

Build your own street signs using your materials. **Number** your signs and put them in the correct order. You can also **draw** your own map of Tinker Town and put your street signs on top of your drawing!

PROJECT 3: DONE!
Get your sticker!

Quantities 0–5 & Writing 0–5

Count how many pieces of fruit are in each basket. Then write the total number in each basket.

Hint! You can cross out each piece of fruit as you count so you don't count anything twice.

Count aloud how many items are in each checkout aisle. The last number you say is the number of objects in the group! Write the total number of items.

Read the poems aloud to count each group. Then write the number of items in the group.

4

Quantities 0–5 & Writing 0–5

I count **1** and **2**.

I count _____ stews.

I count **1**, **2**, and **3**.

I count _____ bags of frozen peas.

I count **1**, **2**, **3**, and **4**.

I count _____ pears in the store.

I count _____ cinnamon bun.
Counting food is a lot of fun!

Can you make your own poems to count up to 5?

TinkerActive Pre-K Math Workbook   29

With the help of an adult, cut out the items below the baskets. Then sort them into groups. How many of each item do you have? Match the number of items to the correct basket by placing the items on top.

The MotMots are buying food for a party! Count the number of items each MotMot wants to buy. Then write the number on the cart.

4

Quantities 0–5 & Writing 0–5

TinkerActive Pre-K Math Workbook

LET'S START!

GATHER THESE TOOLS AND MATERIALS.

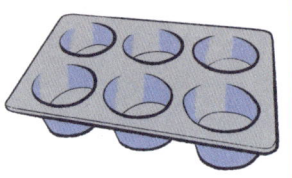 Muffin tin

 A few groups of 1 to 5 small objects, such as: beans, coins, buttons, etc.

 Paper plate

 Sliced bread

 Butter knife (with an adult's help)

 Banana

 Raisins

 Peanut butter

 Marshmallows or grapes

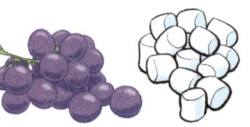 Toothpicks

LET'S TINKER!

Sort your small items into separate spaces of your muffin tin. **Group** the objects that are alike, and then count each group. How many of each item do you have? Are there any other ways you can sort the objects? If so, **sort** them into new groups and count them again!

LET'S MAKE: EDIBLE ART!

1. With the help of an adult, **cut** 1 piece of bread in a curved line.

2. With the help of an adult, **cut** out a small circle from another slice of bread, and then cut that circle in half.

3. Get another slice of bread and spread peanut butter on all the pieces.

4. Assemble the pieces into the shape of a monkey's face on your paper plate. **Place** the curved piece on the bottom of the face, and add the half-circle ears to the sides of the face.

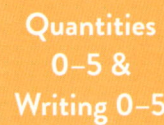

Quantities 0–5 & Writing 0–5

5. With the help of an adult, **cut** four rounds of banana, and cut one of those rounds in half.

6. Add the banana pieces and raisins to make ears, eyes, a nose, and a mouth. Then **enjoy** your edible art!

LET'S ENGINEER!

The MotMots love to build towers all the time—even during snack time! But they only have soft marshmallows and round grapes for snack time today.

How can the MotMots build a tower using their snacks?

Look at your materials. **Think** of a way to build something using the marshmallows that are soft and wobbly, or the grapes that might roll away. How might you keep the snacks steady? How might you build a strong structure?

PROJECT 4: DONE!
Get your sticker!

Follow the path from 0 to 20 with your finger and say each number aloud. Then draw a line from 0 to 20.

Count how many objects are in each group. Then trace the number.

5

Counting to 20

16

17

18

19

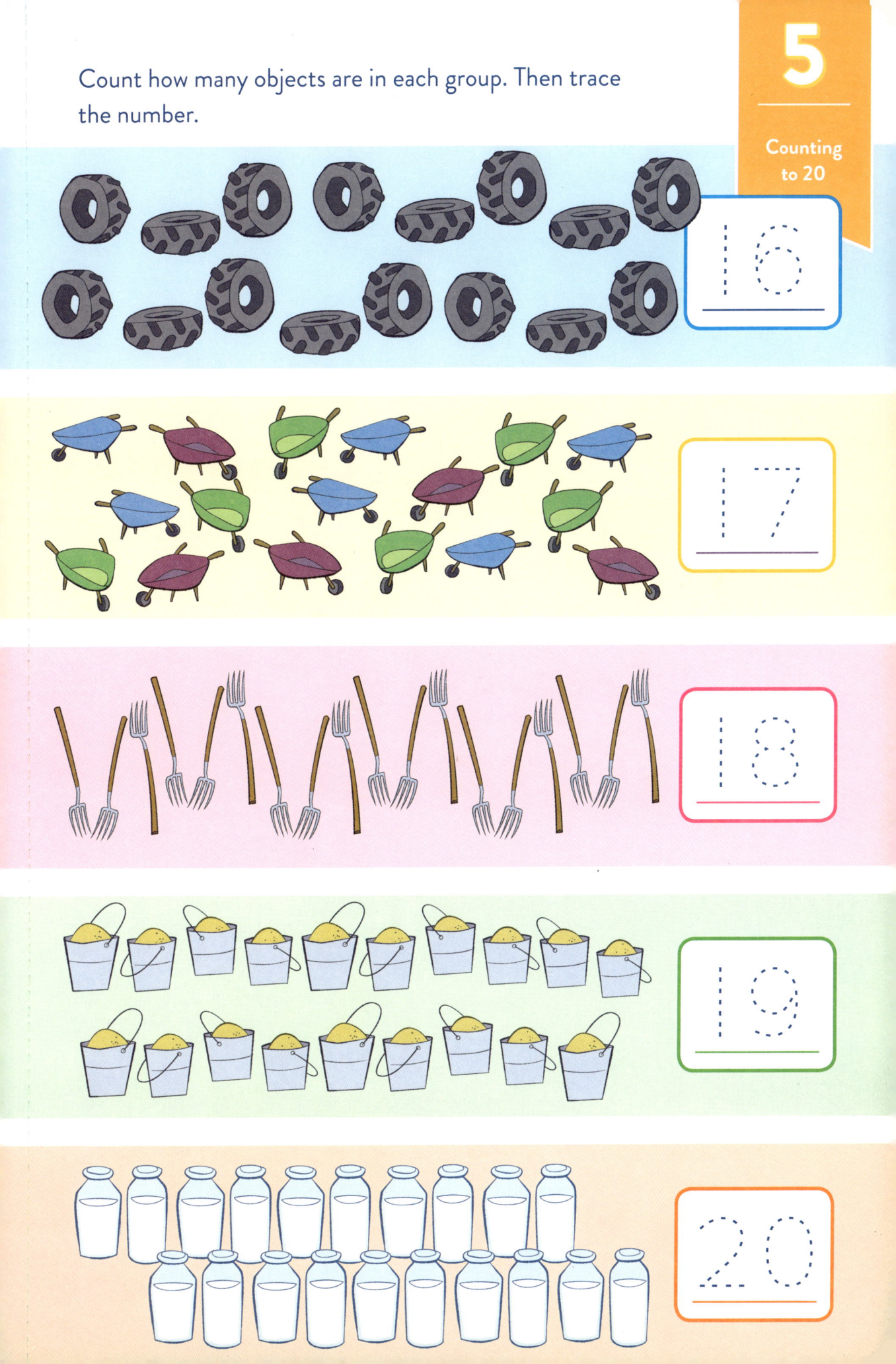

20

Enid loves eating beans. She loves them so much that she planted 19 different bean plants! Follow the path from 0 to 19 with your finger. Then draw a line from 0 to 19 to connect the bean plants.

If Enid planted 1 more bean plant, how many plants would she have?

Color in the correct number of stalls.

5
Counting to 20

11

8

16

19

LET'S START!

GATHER THESE TOOLS AND MATERIALS.

20 rocks	Permanent marker (with an adult's help)	Scissors (with an adult's help)	Construction paper, including black	Glue	White washable paint
Shallow paper bowl or cup	White and black crayons or googly eyes	A few toys or figurines	20 or more craft sticks	Modeling clay	

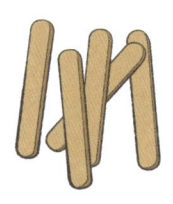

LET'S TINKER!

Make stepping-stones with your materials. With the help of an adult, **write** the numbers 1 through 20 on your rocks with a permanent marker. **Line up** your rocks from 1 through 20 like stepping stones—walk across them if they are large enough, or use your fingers to walk across them if they are small. Every time you step, **count** aloud. Now, **make** a new path in a different shape, without changing the rocks' order. Can you count down and walk from 20 to 1?

40 TinkerActive Pre-K Math Workbook

LET'S MAKE: COUNTING SHEEP!

5

Counting to 20

1. With the help of an adult, **cut out** 4 strips of black construction paper for the sheep's legs, as well as a sheep head and tail.

2. **Glue** the sheep's legs as shown on colored construction paper.

3. **Pour** a small amount of white paint into a shallow bowl or cup.

4. **Dip** your thumb into the white paint and make 20 thumbprints for the sheep's body. **Count** your thumbprints aloud.

5. After the paint dries, **glue** on the face, tail, and googly eyes if you are using them. If you are not using googly eyes, **draw** the eyes.

LET'S ENGINEER!

The baby goats at the farm keep running away and getting into trouble!

How can the MotMots keep the goats safely in one area?

Imagine that your toys or figurines are goats. **Build** something to keep them in one area using 20 craft sticks and your other materials. **Count** your craft sticks aloud as you use them.

PROJECT 5: DONE!
Get your sticker!

LET'S LEARN ABOUT Quantities to 10 & Writing 6–10

Count how many mountain animals are in each group. Then write the total number of animals in each group. (Hint: You can cross out each animal as you count so you don't count any twice.)

_____ yaks

_____ cougars

_____ bears

_____ hares

_____ toads

6
Quantities to 10 & Writing 6–10

___ hawks

___ woodpeckers

___ owls

___ tanagers

___ chickadees

With the help of an adult, fill in the correct answers.

Me By-the-Numbers

My name is _____.

I am _____ years old.

I can't wait to become _____ years old.

There are _____ letters in my name.

I have _____ pets.

My lucky number is _____.

I can count up to _____.

I have _____ siblings.

6

Quantities to 10 & Writing 6–10

This is a drawing of me:

I have _____ fingers.

I have _____ eyes.

I have _____ toes.

Frank is having a picnic for his friends! Read Frank's menu and use the stickers from page 129 to add the correct amount of food for the picnic.

6

7

10

46 TinkerActive Pre-K Math Workbook

Draw a line through the maze so that each MotMot collects the correct number of objects on their hike.

6
Quantities to 10 & Writing 6–10

Dimitri wants to collect **9** leaves.

Callie wants to collect **8** acorns.

Enid wants to collect **10** sticks.

TinkerActive Pre-K Math Workbook 47

LET'S START!

GATHER THESE TOOLS AND MATERIALS.

10 paper cups	 Marker	  10 groups of small items, such as: dice, pretzels, popcorn, etc.	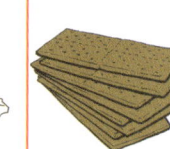 Graham crackers	 Plate
Chocolate	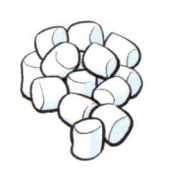 Marshmallows	 Toothpicks or wooden skewers	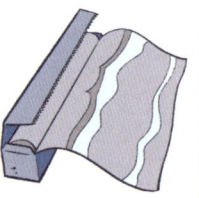 Aluminum foil	 String	 Small figurines

LET'S TINKER!

Turn your paper cups upside down to make "mountains." With the help of an adult, **write** a number from 1 to 10 on each cup. **Separate** your small items into different groups by type and count how many items are in each group. **Match** the grouped items with the number on a cup. **Try** to balance the objects on top of your mountains.

LET'S MAKE: S'MORES!

1. Break a graham cracker into 2 pieces and lay the pieces on a plate.

2. Top 1 cracker with a square of chocolate.

48 TinkerActive Pre-K Math Workbook

3. Top the chocolate with a marshmallow. With the help of an adult, **put** your s'more into an oven or microwave if you would like it heated up.

4. Top with the other graham cracker, press down slightly like a sandwich, and enjoy!

6

Quantities to 10 & Writing 6–10

How many ingredients did you use? How many layers are in the s'more? How many s'mores did you make?

LET'S ENGINEER!

The MotMots were hiking when the wind turned and blew a rainstorm right into Mount Ten! Now they need to take shelter, but there are no caves in sight. They only have sticks, rope, a tarp, and the trees around them.

How can the MotMots stay dry?

Build a mini shelter. What are some materials that are like a tarp and might help cover your figurines so they stay dry? When you are done, **count** how many materials you used for your shelter.

PROJECT 6: DONE!
Get your sticker!

Number Sense

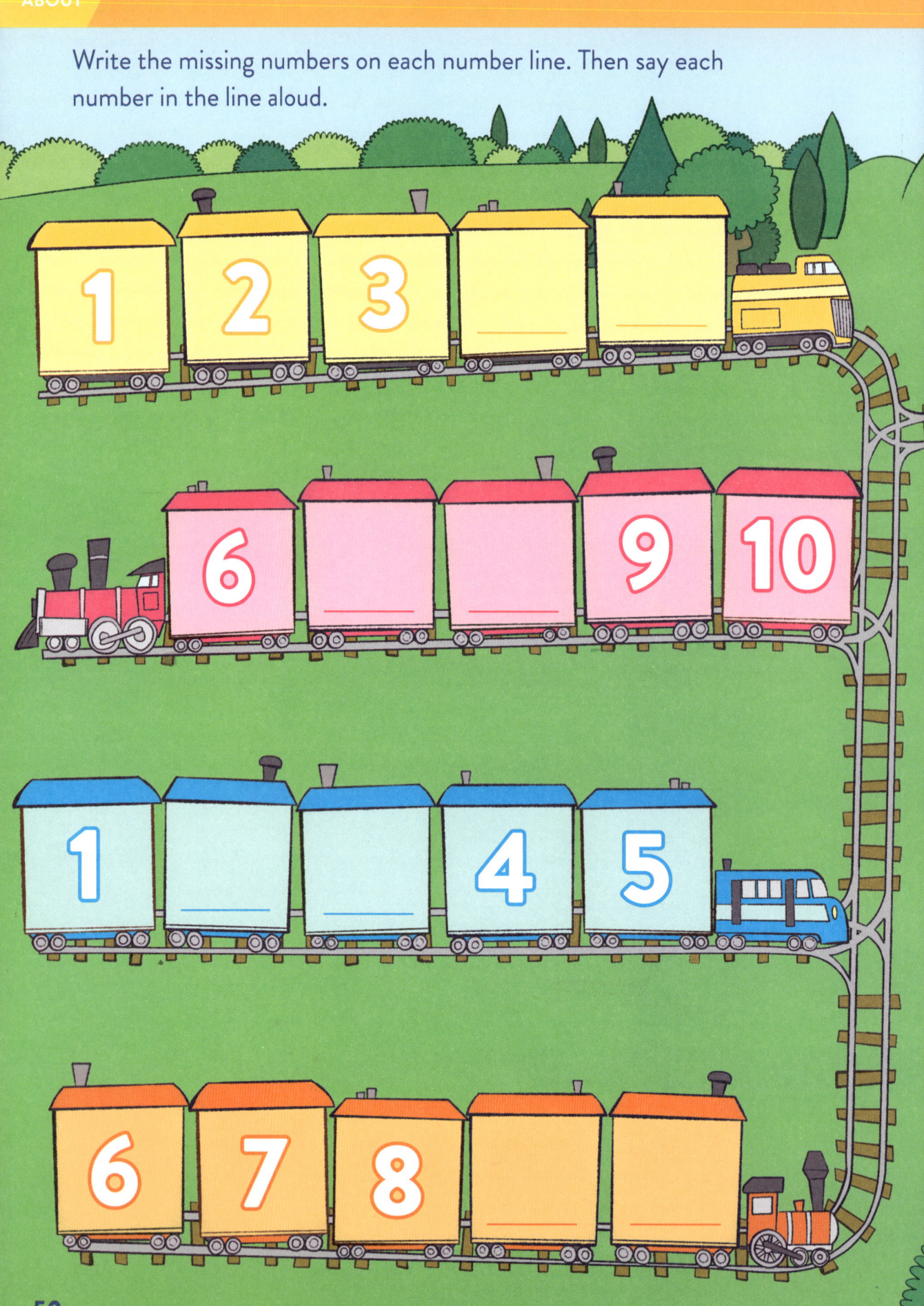

Write the missing numbers on each number line. Then say each number in the line aloud.

1 2 3 ___ ___

6 ___ ___ 9 10

1 ___ ___ 4 5

6 7 8 ___ ___

7

Number Sense

1
2
_
_
5
6
7
_
_
10

Complete the picture by drawing a line from each starting number ★ to 10. Say each number aloud as you go.

Count how many trains are in each group. Then write the number.

3

7

Number Sense

53

Read the number and look at the object. Then sticker the same number of objects along the railroad tracks.

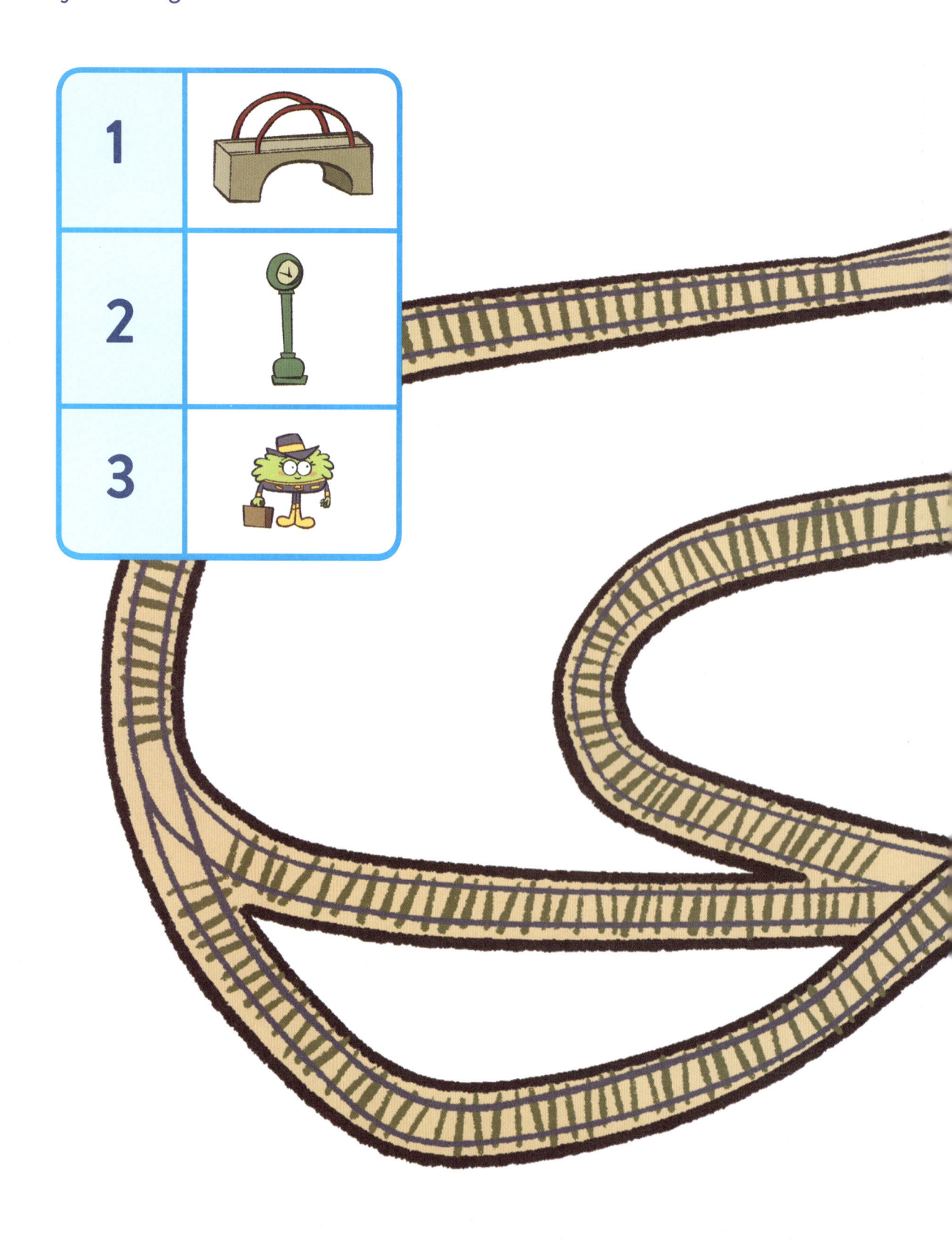

1	
2	
3	

54 TinkerActive Pre-K Math Workbook

7

Number Sense

4	
5	

TinkerActive Pre-K Math Workbook **55**

LET'S START!

GATHER THESE TOOLS AND MATERIALS.

Crayons or markers	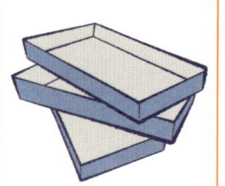 3 or more shoebox lids	 Scissors (with an adult's help)	 Tape	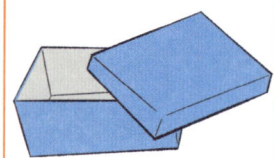 Shoebox	 Toilet paper tube
 Construction paper	  Glue or glue stick	 Small toys	 Cardboard boxes	 Chairs	

LET'S TINKER!

Gather your materials. How many of each type of object do you have? **Arrange** each group in different ways—scattered, in a circle, or in a line. What happens to the number of objects? Does the number change or stay the same when the objects are arranged differently?

LET'S MAKE: LOCOMOTIVE ENGINE!

1. With the help of an adult, **cut** 1 shoebox lid in half widthwise.

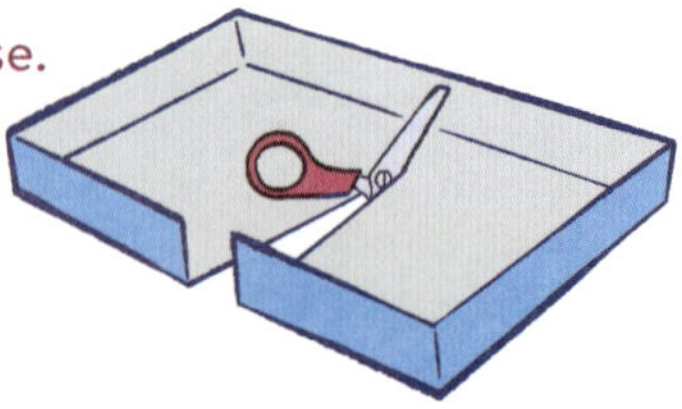

2. With the help of an adult, **cut** a window in each half lid.

56 TinkerActive Pre-K Math Workbook

3. Tape the flat side of the lids to the box.

4. With the help of an adult, **cut** the sides off the remaining shoebox lids.

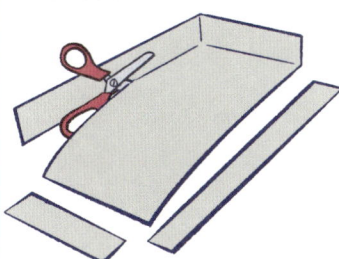

5. Bend the lids slightly so they are curved. Then **tape** them to the shoebox.

7
Number Sense

6. Tape the toilet paper tube on the front for the smokestack.

7. Decorate your locomotive and put your toys in for a ride!

LET'S ENGINEER!

The MotMots in Tinker Town would like to visit their penpals in Bungleburg, but there is a canyon between the two towns.

How can the MotMots visit their friends?

Put two chairs a small distance apart to act as your cliffs. The ground in between is the bottom of your canyon! Then **build** a bridge between them using your materials. **Make** the bridge large enough for your shoebox train to cross. Then **test** it out! Will the bridge hold your train? **Put** some items in your train. **Count** them aloud as you place them inside. How many items can you add before your bridge breaks?

PROJECT 7: DONE!
Get your sticker!

Addition Up to 5

LET'S LEARN ABOUT

Count how many toys are in each row. Say the number aloud. Next, draw one more toy in each row. How many toys are there now? Write the number.

8

Addition Up to 5

Count how many toys are in each column. Say the number aloud. Then follow the directions.

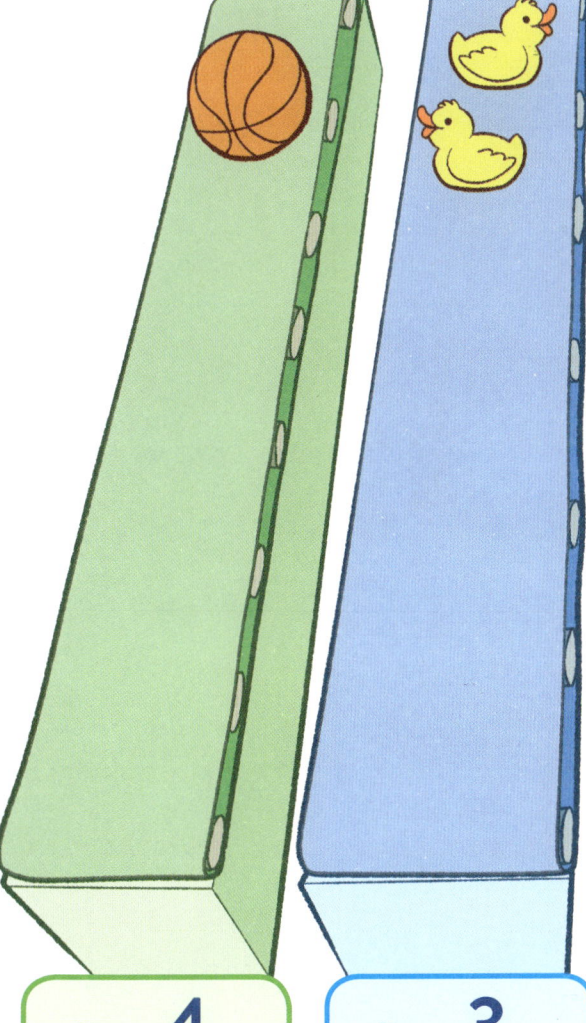

Draw **4** more balls. Count the balls again. How many balls are there now? Write the number.

Draw **3** more ducks. Count the ducks again. How many ducks are there now? Write the number.

Draw **2** more drums. Count the drums again. How many drums are there now? Write the number.

Draw **1** more top. Count the tops again. How many tops are there now? Write the number.

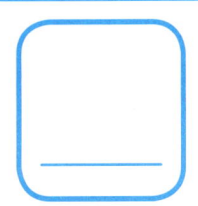

TinkerActive Pre-K Math Workbook 59

Count how many fingers are showing on each hand below. How many fingers are there in all? Say the number aloud and write the number.

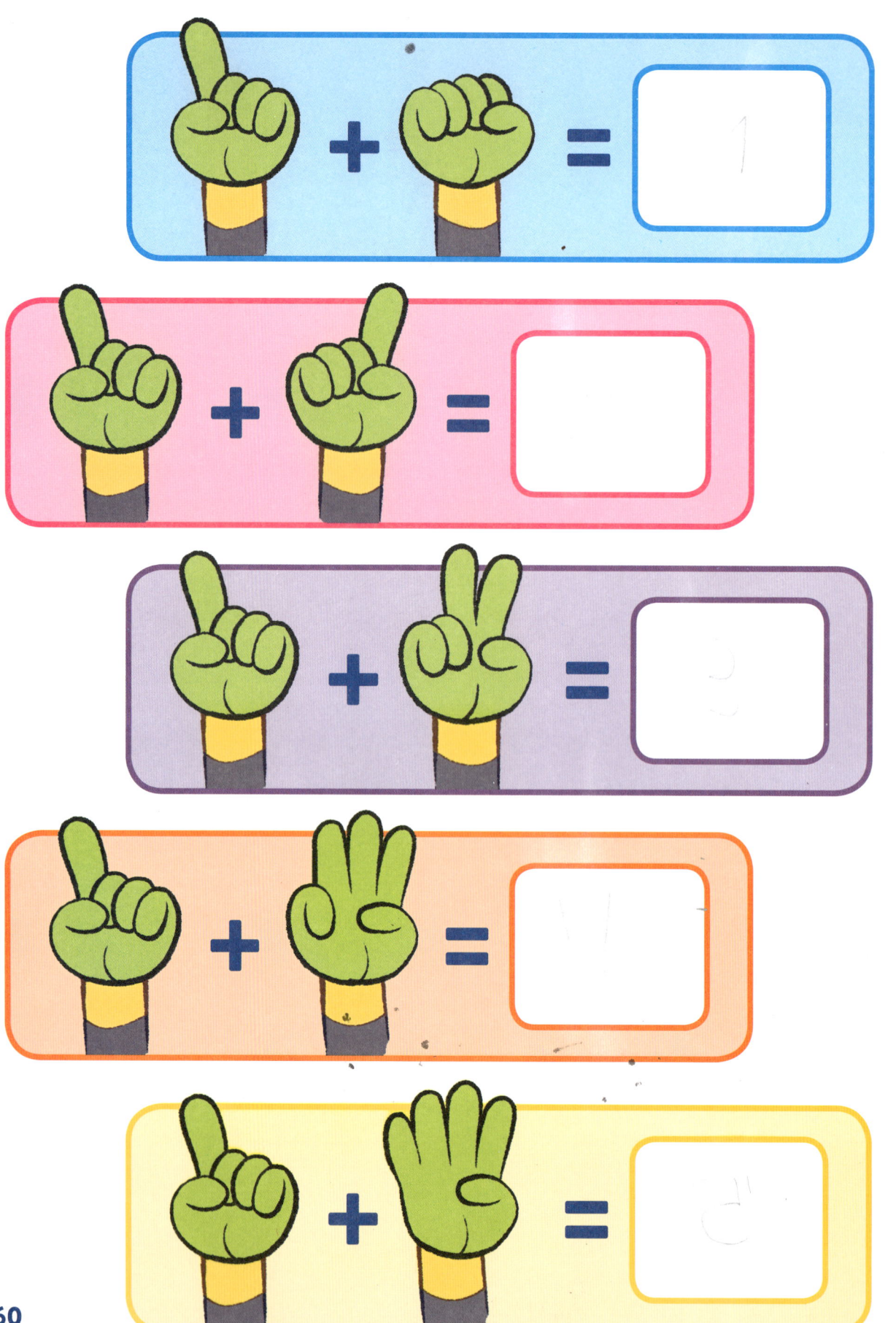

8

Addition Up to 5

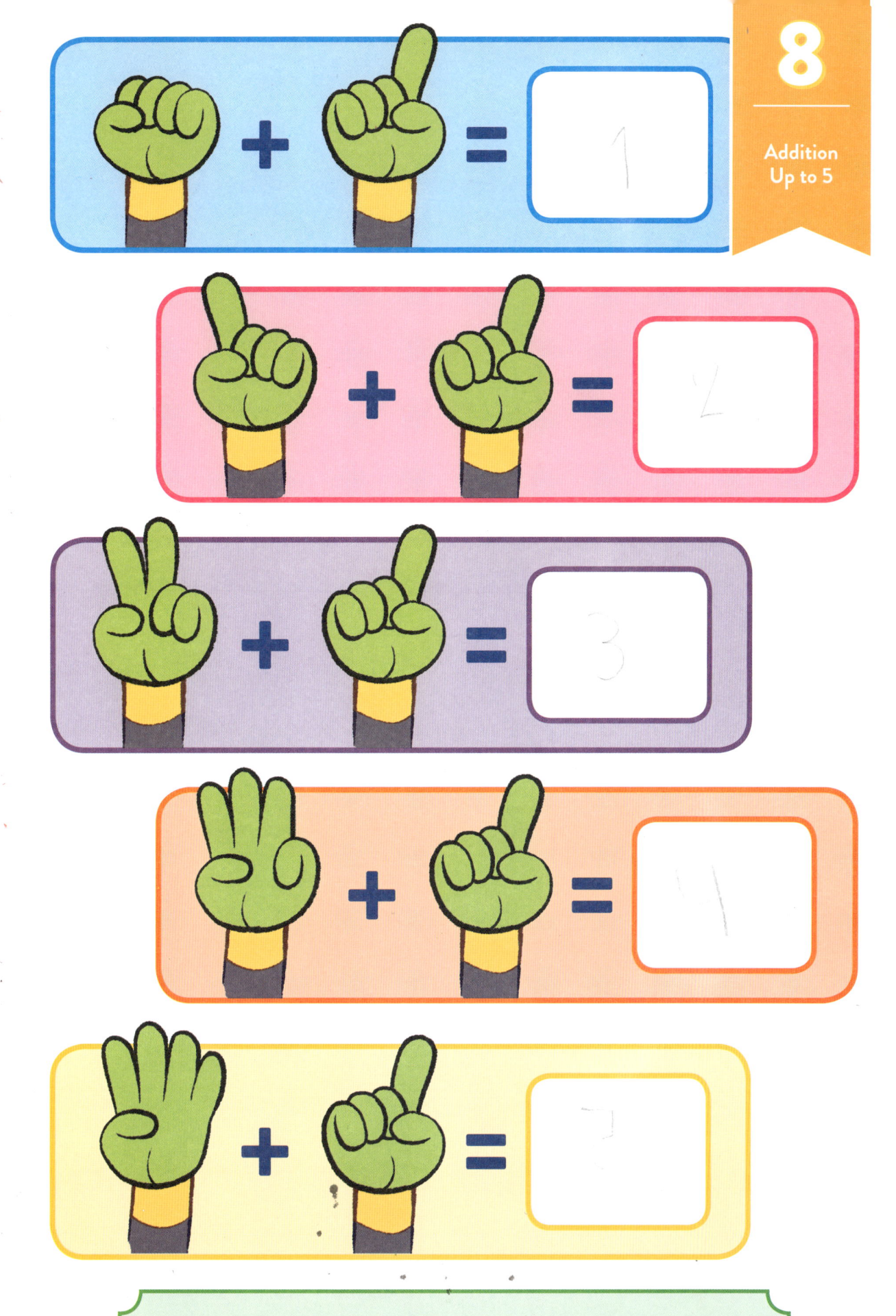

0 + 1 = 1

1 + 1 = 2

2 + 1 = 3

3 + 1 = 4

4 + 1 = 5

Use your own hands to add! Copy the MotMot hands and count your own fingers. How many fingers are there in all?

61

Read about the toys each MotMot is making. Then answer each question.

Enid paints 1 train. Then she paints 2 more. How many trains does she paint in all?

1 + 2 = ___

Brian folds 2 paper airplanes. Then he folds 1 more. How many airplanes does he fold in all?

2 + 1 = ___

Frank makes 3 dolls. Then he makes 2 more. How many dolls does he make in all?

3 + 2 = ___

Dimitri makes 2 kites. Then he makes 3 more. How many kites does he make in all?

2 + 3 = ___

Count how many toys are in each group. Then count how many toys there are in all. Last, write the numbers and, with the help of an adult, read the number sentences aloud.

8

Addition Up to 5

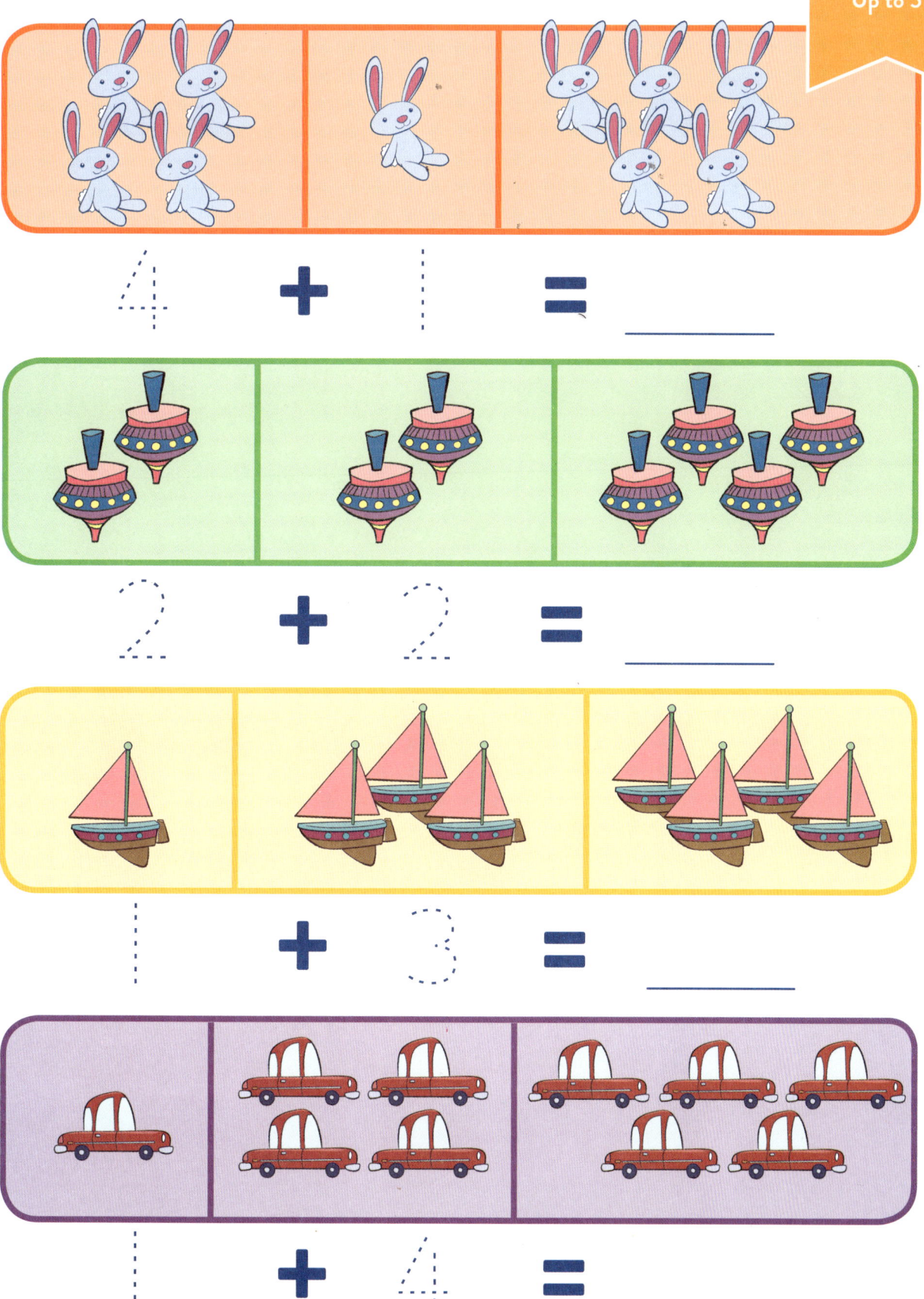

4 + 1 = ___

2 + 2 = ___

___ + 3 = ___

___ + 4 = ___

63

LET'S START!

GATHER THESE TOOLS AND MATERIALS.

| 2 small toys |  2 small books | 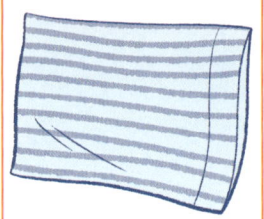 Pillowcase or bag |  Crayons or markers |  Paper bowl |

| Paper towel roll |  Scissors (with an adult's help) |  6 or more paper plates |  Toilet paper roll |

LET'S TINKER!

Count how many toys you have. Now, **count** how many books you have. **Put** 1 book in the pillowcase. How many books are inside the pillowcase? **Add** a toy to the pillowcase. How many objects are inside now? **Add** the other book and toy until they are all inside. How many are there in all? When you put the 2 groups together in the pillowcase, is the group bigger or smaller than when they were separate?

LET'S MAKE: RING TOSS TOY!

1. **Trace** the end of the paper towel tube onto the bottom of a paper bowl.

2. With the help of an adult, **cut** the circle out of the bowl to create a hole.

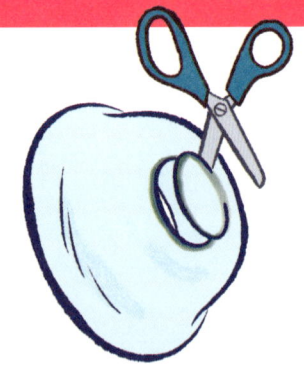

3. Fit the paper towel tube into the hole to make a stake.

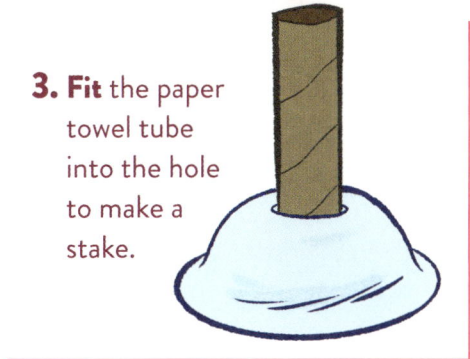

4. With the help of an adult, **cut** the center out of 6 paper plates to make your rings.

8

Addition Up to 5

5. Color and decorate 3 rings one way. Then **color** and decorate. 3 rings another way.

6. Find a partner and play! Each player chooses their own ring color, and then takes turns, throwing one ring at a time until all of them have been thrown. **Score** 2 points for each ringer and 1 point for any ring touching the stake. **Pick up** the rings and continue playing until one player reaches 5 points.

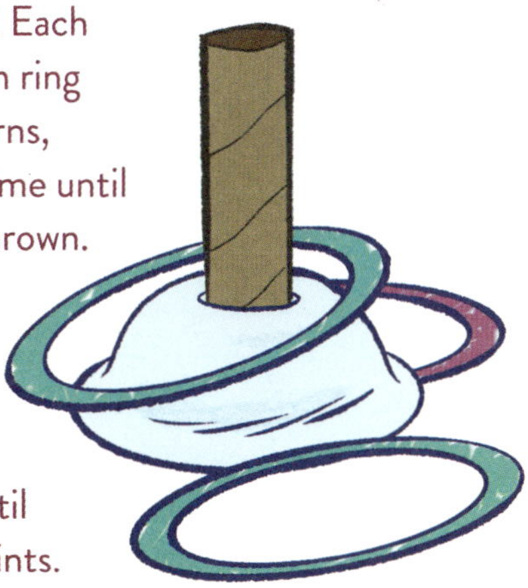

LET'S ENGINEER!

Frank and Brian were playing ring toss, but the game was too hard! Neither MotMot could get their rings around the stake.

How can the MotMots make the game easier?

Make your ring toss toy easier. **Try** bringing the stake closer, adding more rings so each player gets more tries, making a shorter stake, or changing the rules of the game completely! What other ways can you make it easier? Once you think of a new way to play, **ask** another person to play. At the end of each game, **count** each person's points to find out who won. You can also **add** your points together. How many points do you have in all? Can you break your record? **Play** again!

PROJECT 8: DONE!
Get your sticker!

Subtraction Under 5

How many balloons does each MotMot have? Count them aloud, then cross out 1 balloon in each group to pop it. How many balloons are left? Count the remaining balloons and write the number.

How many white balloons does each MotMot have? Count them aloud, then color 1 balloon in each group. How many white balloons are left? Write the number.

9

Subtraction Under 5

TinkerActive Pre-K Math Workbook 67

The MotMots are playing Enid Says Subtract. Read the prompt aloud and use your fingers to subtract. Then write the number.

ENID SAYS SUBTRACT 1 FROM 5.

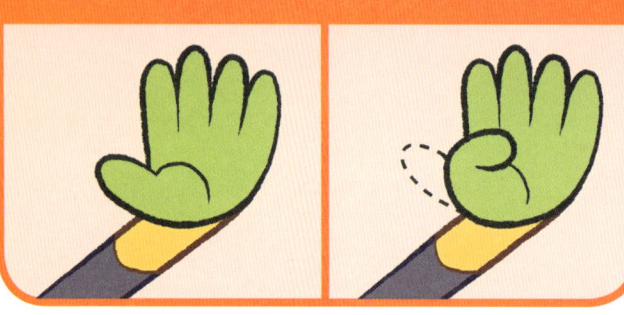

5 − 1 = 4

ENID SAYS SUBTRACT 2 FROM 5.

5 − 2 = ___

ENID SAYS SUBTRACT 2 FROM 3.

3 − 2 = ___

9
Subtraction Under 5

ENID SAYS SUBTRACT 1 FROM 4.

4 − 1 = _____

ENID SAYS SUBTRACT 4 FROM 5.

5 − 4 = _____

ENID SAYS SUBTRACT 3 FROM 5.

5 − 3 = _____

How many fingers should be up to begin? How many fingers should you put down? The number of fingers that are left up is your answer!

Read about the food each MotMot ate at Tinker Town's annual barbecue. Then write the answer to each question.

There were 5 hot dogs. Frank ate 2. How many hot dogs were left?

5   -   2   =   ___

There were 3 hamburgers. Enid ate 2. How many hamburgers were left?

3   -   2   =   ___

There was 1 cup of lemonade. Brian drank it. How many cups of lemonade were left?

1   -   1   =   ___

Count the food on each plate aloud. Then trace the missing numbers. Last, say aloud and write how much food was left over.

9

Subtraction Under 5

3 - 1 = ___

4 - 2 = ___

2 - 1 = ___

5 - 4 = ___

TinkerActive Pre-K Math Workbook 71

LET'S START!

GATHER THESE TOOLS AND MATERIALS.

- 5 crayons or markers
- Empty rectangular tissue box 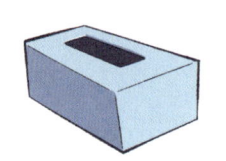
- Green paint or green construction paper 
- Scissors (with an adult's help) 
- White construction paper 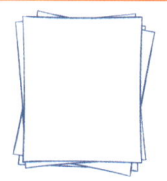
- Glue or glue stick 
- Up to 5 small snacks such as popcorn, nuts, mini pretzels, etc. 
- Cardboard boxes 
- Tape 

LET'S TINKER!

Play Hide-and-Seek Subtraction! **Get** a partner and count how many crayons or markers you have. Now **ask** your partner to hide one. How many are left? **Find** the missing object and put it back with the rest. How many do you have in all? **Play** again by hiding 2, 3, 4, or all 5 crayons or markers.

LET'S MAKE: HUNGRY AMELIA!

1. **Paint** your tissue box green or cover it with green construction paper. **Let** dry.

2. With the help of an adult, **cut** the edge of the white construction paper for Amelia's teeth. Then **draw** and cut Amelia's eyeballs and cheeks.

3. **Glue** the teeth to the bottom of the tissue box right inside the opening.

4. **Glue** Amelia's eyeballs and rosy cheeks.

5. **Feed** Amelia! **Count** how many snacks you have. Then **feed** Amelia 1 snack. How many snacks are left? **Keep feeding** Amelia 1 snack at a time and count how many are left. Can you feed her all the snacks so there are none left?

9

Subtraction Under 5

LET'S ENGINEER!

Every year Frank makes 4 apple pies for the Tinker Town barbecue. And every year, 2 pies go missing!

How can Frank protect his pies?

Draw 4 apple pies on paper and, with the help of an adult, cut them out. If 2 pies go missing, how many are left? **Build** something to protect your remaining pies!

PROJECT 9: DONE!
Get your sticker!

Comparing Quantities

LET'S LEARN ABOUT

Count how many objects are in each cubby. Then circle the group that has **more** in each row.

1   4

2   3

5   3

4   3

Count how many objects are in each cubby. Then circle the group that has **less** in each row.

10

Comparing Quantities

1	4
4	3
3	5
5	2

TinkerActive Pre-K Math Workbook 75

Draw lines to pair the objects. Are there **more**, **less**, or the **same** number of each group of objects? Finish each sentence by circling the correct answer.

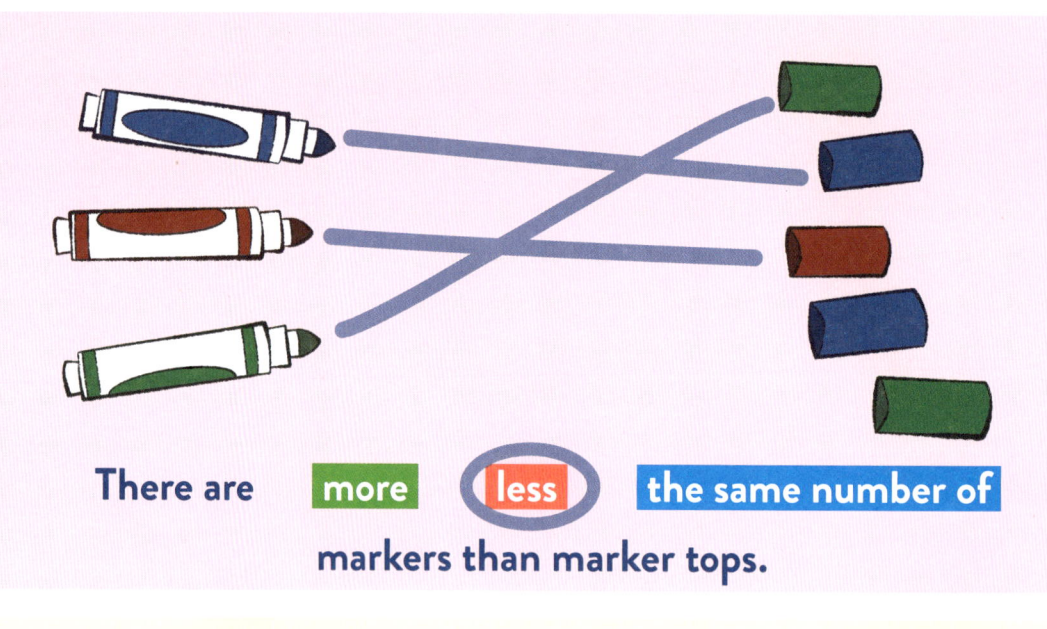

There are   more   (less)   the same number of markers than marker tops.

There are   more   less   the same number of chairs than desks.

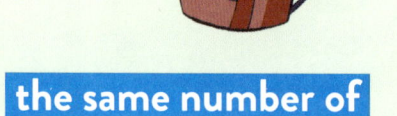

There are   more   less   the same number of books as backpacks.

10

Comparing Quantities

There are [more] [less] [the same number of] sandwiches than lunch boxes.

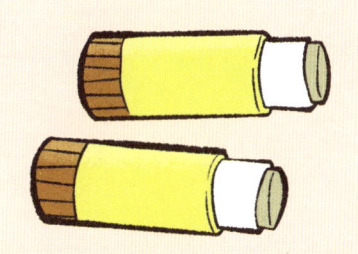

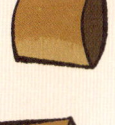

There are [more] [less] [the same number of] glue sticks as glue tops.

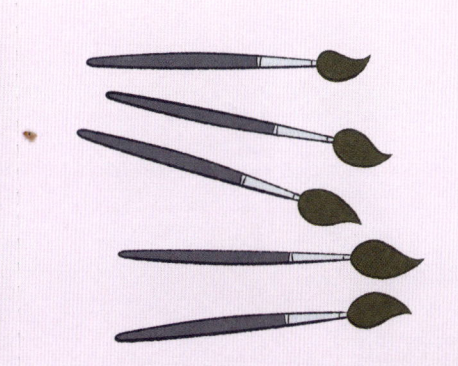

There are [more] [less] [the same number of] paintbrushes than paint bottles.

TinkerActive Pre-K Math Workbook **77**

Count how many snacks each MotMot has aloud. Draw lines through the maze so each MotMot gets more of his or her snack.

Now how many snacks does each MotMot have in all? Say it aloud.

78 TinkerActive Pre-K Math Workbook

Add stickers from page 129 so each pair of MotMots has the same number of snacks.

10

Comparing Quantities

LET'S START!

GATHER THESE TOOLS AND MATERIALS.

1 to 5 paper cups	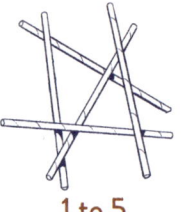 1 to 5 drinking straws	 Pillowcase	 Paper plate	 Scissors (with an adult's help)	 Crayons
 Brad	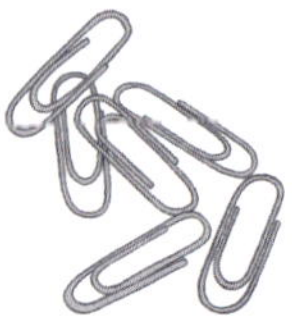 Paper clips	 Small snacks, like nuts, popcorn, baby carrots, etc.	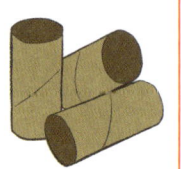 4 toilet paper rolls	Small piece of cardboard or cereal box	 Stuffed animal

LET'S TINKER!

Count how many paper cups and straws you have. Do you have more of one or the other? Or do you have the same number of cups and straws? Now, **test** it out! **Gather** your paper cups and straws in the pillowcase and shake it up. **Pull** 1 item out at a time and match each cup with a straw. **Keep matching** until your pillowcase is empty. Does every cup have a matching straw?

LET'S MAKE: SPINNING SNACKS!

1. With the help of an adult, **poke** a small hole in the center of the paper plate using scissors.

2. **Draw** 3 lines from the center of the paper plate, like so:

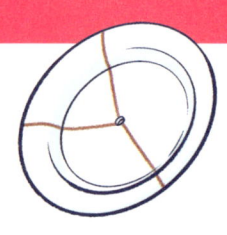

3. In different sections **write** "More," "Less," or "Same," like so:

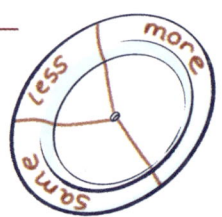

80 TinkerActive Pre-K Math Workbook

10

Comparing Quantities

4. **Poke** a brad through the hole in the paper plate. **Bend** the back side of the brad so the paper plate can move and so a paper clip can fit.

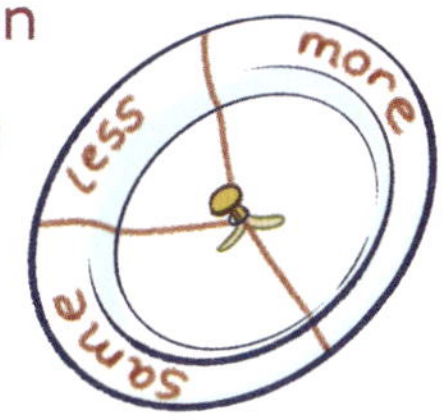

5. **Attach** the paper clip to the brad. It should spin freely.

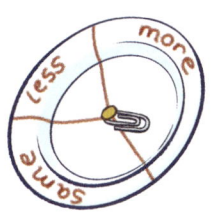

6. **Get** a friend or family member and play Spinning Snacks! **Choose** a snack as the prize. Then **spin** the paper clip. **Read** the word where the paper clip stops. If you **land** on "More" then you can take more snacks than the other player. If you **land** on "Less," take less, and if you land on "Same," share the snacks equally. Next, it's your partner's turn to **pick** a snack and spin!

LET'S ENGINEER!

Dimitri wants to have snack time with his 3 favorite stuffed bears—but he only has enough stools for himself and 2 of the bears.

How can Dimitri sit with all the bears?

Build a stool for your own stuffed animal. Once your stuffed animal can sit, **share** some snacks. **Count out** the snacks so everyone gets the same amount. Then enjoy your snacks together!

PROJECT 10: DONE!
Get your sticker!

Measurement

LET'S LEARN ABOUT

Circle the object that is **bigger** in each row. Then underline the object that is **smaller**.

Circle the object that is **taller** in each scene. Then underline the object that is **shorter**.

11 Measurement

83

Circle the object that is **longer** in each row. Then underline the object that is **shorter**.

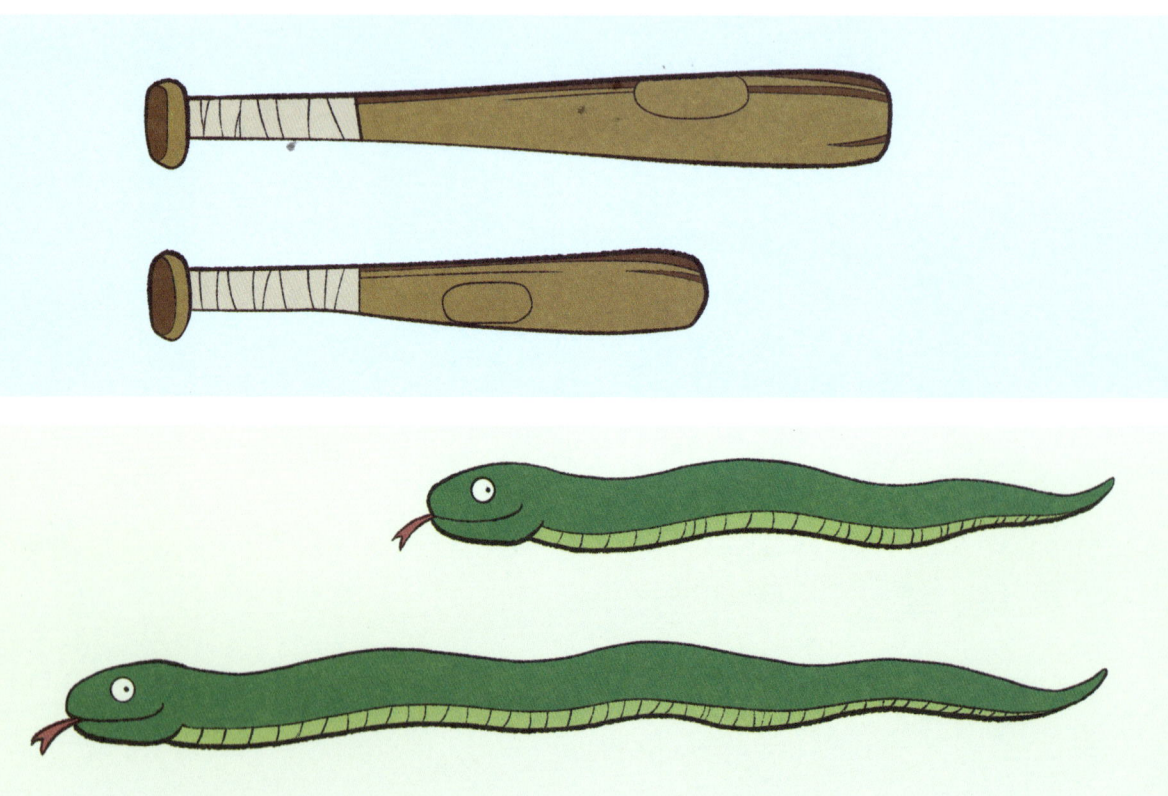

Circle the object that is **heavier** in each box. Then underline the object that is **lighter**.

11

Measurement

Circle the **tallest** MotMot in each row. Underline the **shortest** MotMot in each row.

AMELIA BRIAN FRANK

DIMITRI ENID CALLIE

With the help of an adult, cut out the MotMots on page 86. Then place each MotMot next to the ride entrance. Which MotMots can ride on the roller coaster? Say their names aloud.

11

Measurement

You must be **THIS ▶ TALL** to ride

LET'S START!

GATHER THESE TOOLS AND MATERIALS.

- Toys of various sizes, such as vehicles, instruments, blocks, etc.
- Scissors (with an adult's help) 
- Optional: hole puncher 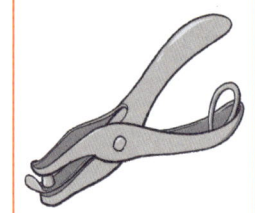
- 2 paper cups 
- 2 pieces of string (about 12 inches long) 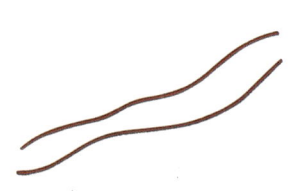
- Plastic hanger with hooks or notches 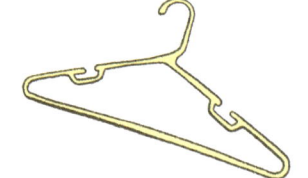
- 3 strings of various lengths 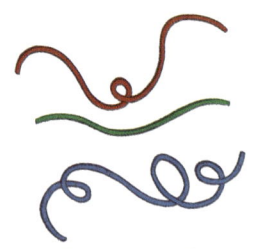
- Tape 

LET'S TINKER!

Arrange your toys by size—from biggest to smallest, or smallest to biggest. What if you arrange the toys only by height? Will your arrangement change? Why or why not? **Try** arranging by length and weight, too. How many other ways can you arrange your toys?

LET'S MAKE: TOY SCALE!

1. With the help of an adult, **use** your hole puncher or scissors to punch a hole through both sides of a paper cup.

2. With the help of an adult, **tie** the ends of a 12-inch piece of string to the holes in the cup.

88 TinkerActive Pre-K Math Workbook

3. **Repeat** steps 1 and 2 with the other cup and 12-inch string—these are the buckets for your scale!

11

Measurement

4. **Place** the string into the notches or hooks of the hanger so the cups hang down.

5. **Place** the hanger where it can swing easily, like on a shower rod or drying rack.

6. **Weigh** your toys! **Put** a different toy in each bucket. Which bucket hangs lower than the other? Which toy weighs more? **Compare** all your toys.

LET'S ENGINEER!

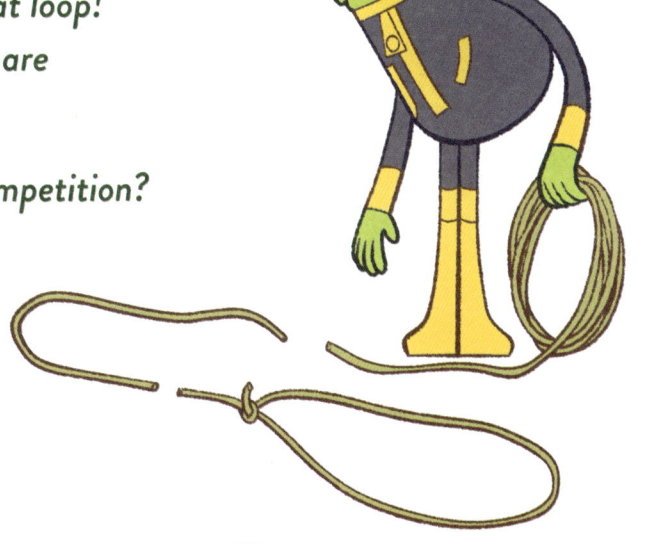

Dimitri wants to enter the lasso trick competition—he can do a great flat loop! But his lasso broke and the pieces are too short to finish the trick!

How can Dimitri still enter the competition?

Look at your remaining pieces of string. How can you make them longer? Can you put them back together somehow?

PROJECT 11: DONE!
Get your sticker!

Units of Measurement

LET'S LEARN ABOUT

Look at each crane. Then draw buildings that are as **tall** as each crane.

Look at each pipe. Then draw metal beams that are as **long** as each pipe.

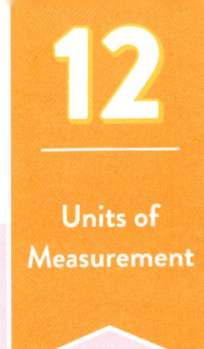

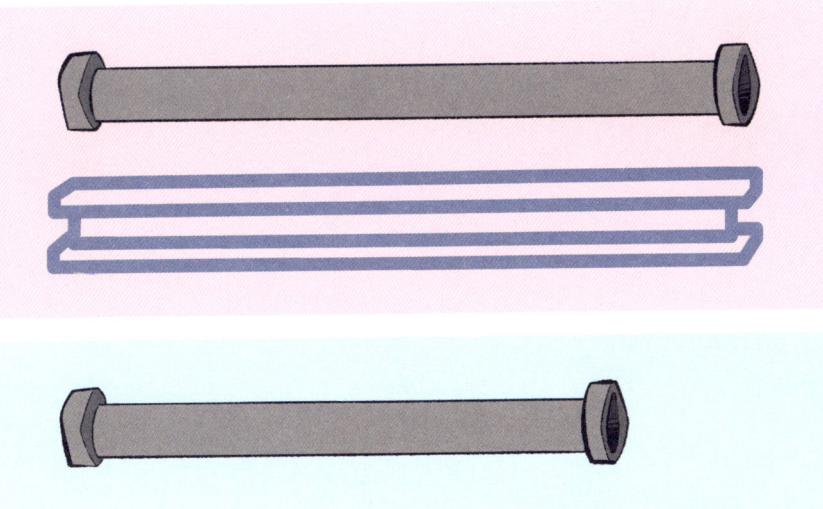

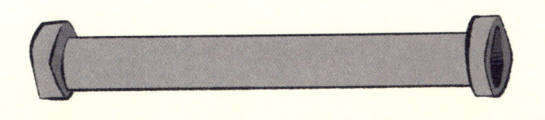

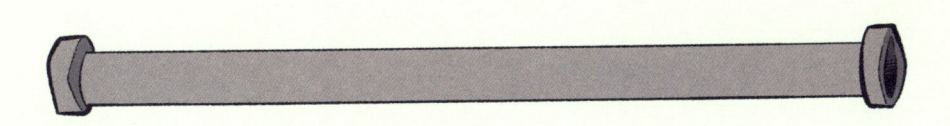

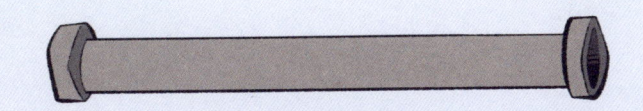

12

Units of Measurement

How **tall** is each stack of bricks? Count aloud how many bricks are in each stack. Then write the number.

How **long** is each track of carts? Count aloud how many carts are on each track. Then write the number.

12

Units of Measurement

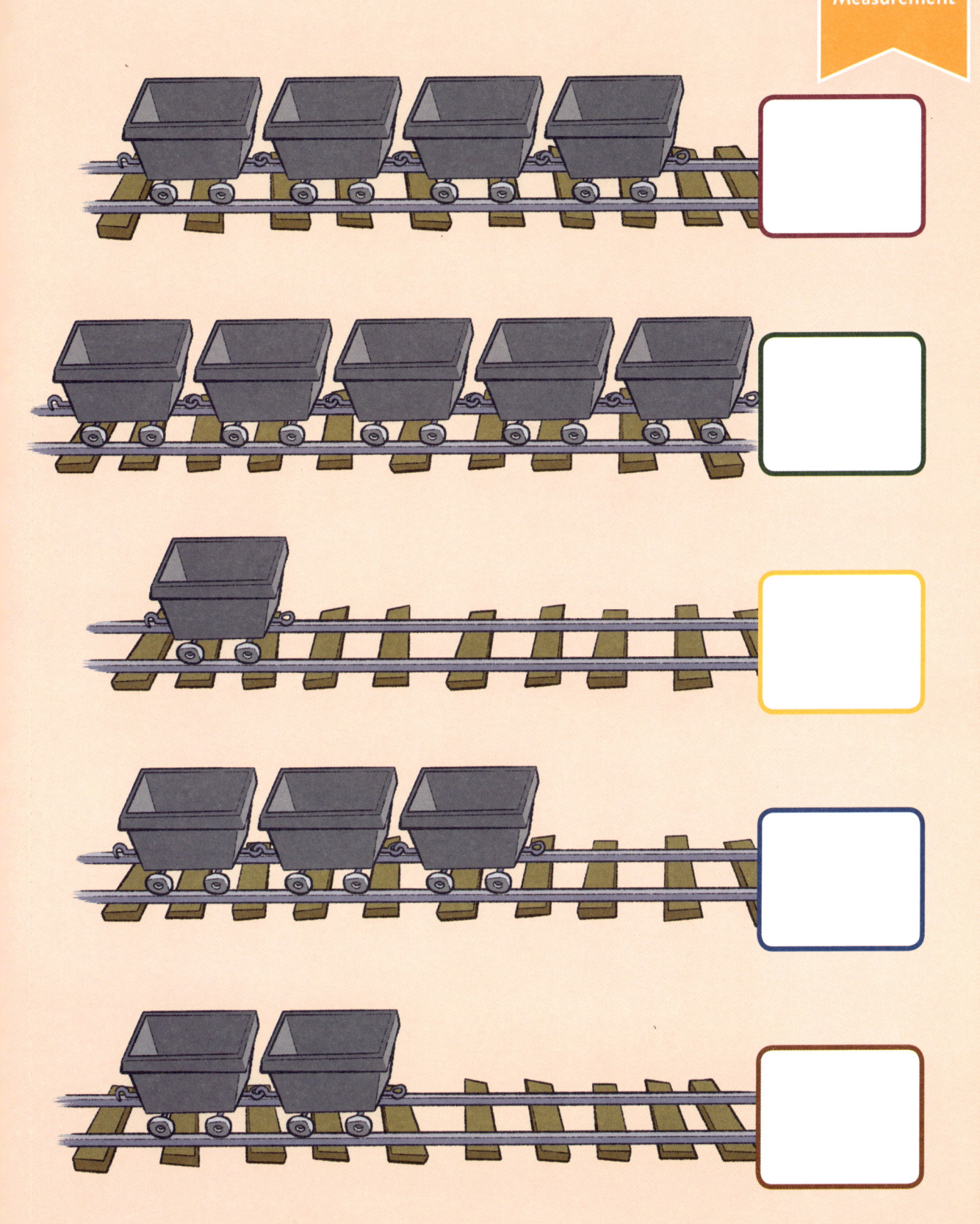

How many bricks **tall** is each object? Count how many bricks are beside each object. Then write the number.

How many bricks **long** is each object? Count how many bricks are underneath each object. Then write the number.

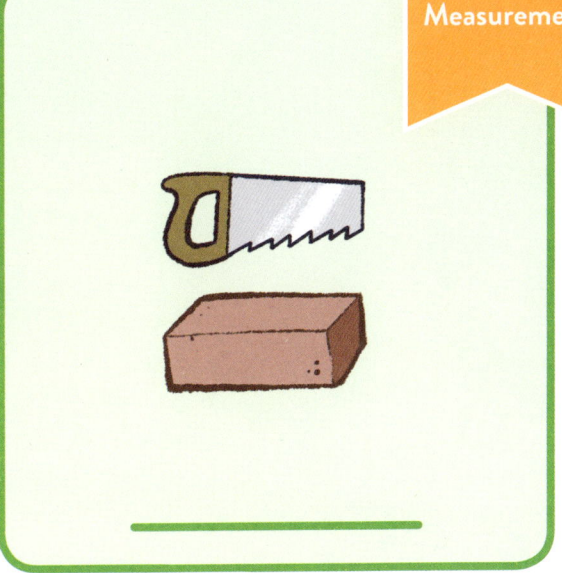

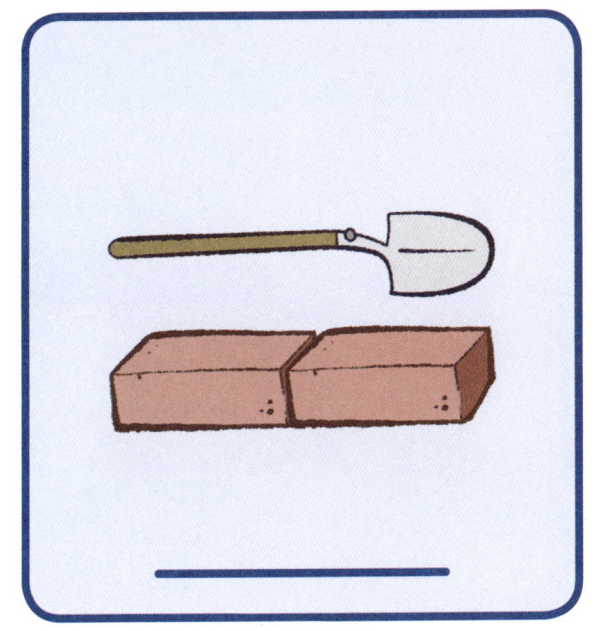

12
Units of Measurement

LET'S START!

GATHER THESE TOOLS AND MATERIALS.

5 identical blocks	 Crayon	 1 toilet paper tube	 String	 Tape	 Construction paper

Scissors (with an adult's help)	 2 paper towel tubes	 Chairs	 Sheets	 Pillows or sofa cushions

LET'S TINKER!

Go on a measurement hunt! **Find** objects that are 1 block tall, 2 blocks tall, 3 blocks tall, 4 blocks tall, and 5 blocks tall. If you can't find an object that is the correct height, **draw** one or make your own. Then **do** the same for length! **Find** objects that are 1 block long, 2 blocks long, and so on.

LET'S MAKE: PAPER CRANE!

1. With the help of an adult, **cut** a toilet paper tube in half widthwise.

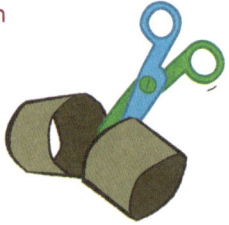

2. **Run** the string through the tube and tape it in place. This is your basket!

3. With the help of an adult, **draw** and cut a triangle out of construction paper to make the top of your crane.

4. **Tape** the string of your basket to an end of the triangle.

12

Units of Measurement

5. With the help of an adult, **make** two cuts across from each other on one end of the paper towel roll.

6. **Insert** the top of your crane in the cuts and stand your crane up. Can your crane hold any of your materials?

LET'S ENGINEER!

The tunnel in Tinker Town's park collapsed! The MotMots have to build a new tunnel. But first, they need to know how tall to make it so that MotMots can walk through.

How can the MotMots find out how tall to make the new tunnel?

Plan and build a tunnel that you can walk through using pillows, sheets, and chairs. How tall must your tunnel be? What can you use to measure the height of your body? How can you make sure the sides of your tunnel are the right height?

PROJECT 12: DONE!
Get your sticker!

LET'S LEARN ABOUT

Spatial Reasoning

Color the books on the top shelf **red**. Then color the books on the bottom shelf **blue**.

98 TinkerActive Pre-K Math Workbook

Circle the MotMots that are **in front** of the bookshelves.
Underline the MotMots that are **next to** the bookshelves.

13

Spatial Reasoning

Find the MotMots that are **behind** the bookshelves. How many are there? Say the number aloud.

Circle the MotMots that are walking **up** the stairs. Underline the MotMots that are walking **down** the stairs.

Get the MotMot stickers from page 129. Place the MotMots **on** the carpet for story time!

13

Spatial Reasoning

Find the MotMots **in** the reading nooks. How many are there? Say the number aloud.

If you wrote a book, what would you write about? First, draw a picture of what you would like to write about. Then write 1 word about your book **above** your picture. Last, write your name **under** your picture.

My Book About

_____

by _____

Circle the MotMot that is **first** in each line. Then underline the MotMot that is **last** in each line.

13

Spatial Reasoning

TinkerActive Pre-K Math Workbook 103

LET'S START!

GATHER THESE TOOLS AND MATERIALS.

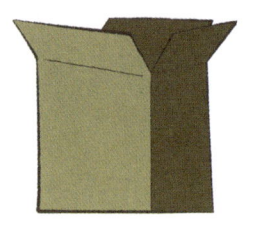

- Large cardboard box
- 10 craft sticks 
- Tape 
- Paint and paintbrush 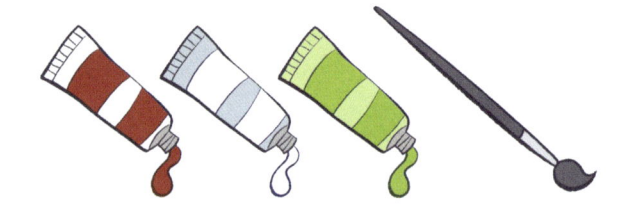
- Scissors (with an adult's help) 

LET'S TINKER!

Get your cardboard box and act out each location: go **in front of** your box, go **behind** it, go **next to** it, and then go **inside** it. Is it still a box each time? Maybe it's a cave once you're inside it! Maybe it's the counter of an ice cream shop when you're next to it! What other ways can you move around your box?

LET'S MAKE: YOUR PERSONAL PUZZLE!

1. **Place** your craft sticks side by side and tape them together with 2 or 3 pieces of tape.

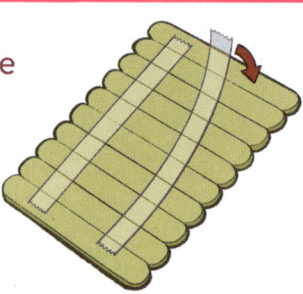

104 TinkerActive Pre-K Math Workbook

2. Flip the sticks over so the tape is on the bottom, and paint a picture on them. This will be your puzzle.

3. Wait for the paint to dry. Then **remove** the tape.

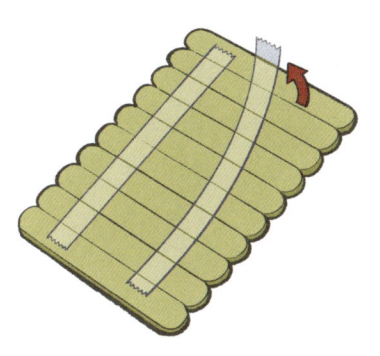

13

Spatial Reasoning

4. Move and mix up your puzzle parts! Can you put your painting back together? Which craft stick is first? Which is last? Which ones are in the middle?

LET'S ENGINEER!

Brian wants to go to the library, but he has to put his shoes on first. The problem is, he can't remember which is his left shoe and which is his right shoe!

How can Brian remember which shoe goes on which foot?

Get a pair of your own shoes. How do you tell which is the shoe for your left foot and which is for your right foot? **Use** your materials and the stickers on page 129 to help you know which shoe goes on which foot.

PROJECT 13: DONE!
Get your sticker!

LET'S LEARN ABOUT 2D Shapes

A **square** is a flat shape with 4 sides that are the same length, as well as 4 corners.

A **rectangle** is a flat shape with 2 longer sides and 2 shorter sides, as well as 4 corners.

Use your finger to trace the **rectangles** and **squares** in each painting. Count the number of sides aloud as you trace.

Draw your own rectangle or square on the blank canvas. Count the number of sides aloud as you draw. Then color in your art!

106 TinkerActive Pre-K Math Workbook

Find the rectangles and squares in the painting and sculpture. Then color in the shapes.

14

2D Shapes

How many sides does a rectangle have?

How many sides does a square have?

A **triangle** is a flat shape with 3 sides.

Trace the **triangles** on the mobile. Count the number of sides aloud as you trace.

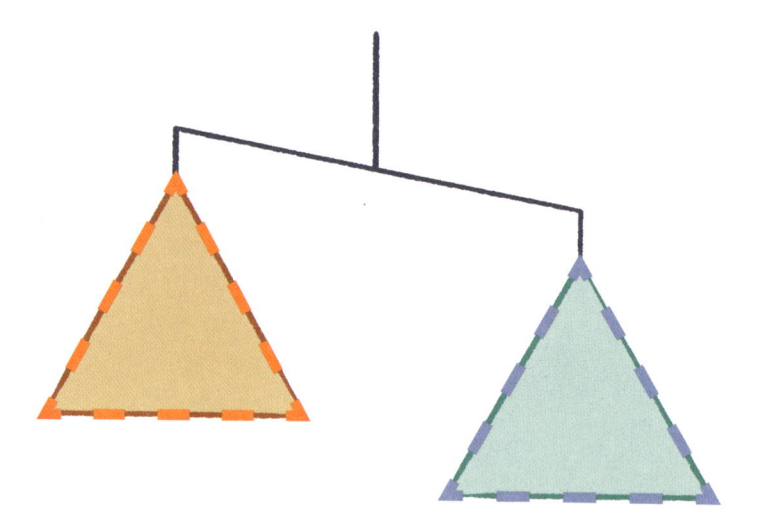

Draw your own triangles on the empty mobile. Count the number of sides aloud as you draw. Then color your triangle art!

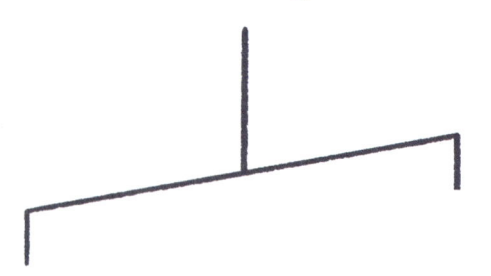

How many sides does a triangle have?

108 TinkerActive Pre-K Math Workbook

Circle each piece of art that has a triangle in it.

14

2D Shapes

A **circle** is a flat shape made by a curved line. It has no sides.
Trace each **circle**. Describe the shape aloud as you trace.

How many sides does a circle have?

Draw and color your own circle on the empty pedestal!

110 TinkerActive Pre-K Math Workbook

Draw lines to match the objects to their shapes. Then say the shapes aloud.

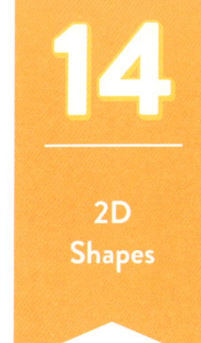

circle

rectangle

triangle

Find objects around you that are shaped like rectangles, squares, circles, and triangles. Then draw them below.

14

2D Shapes

TinkerActive Pre-K Math Workbook 111

LET'S START! GATHER THESE TOOLS AND MATERIALS.

- Scissors (with an adult's help)
- Construction paper 
- Glue stick 
- Optional: decorative items such as ribbon, beads, feathers, etc. 
- White paper 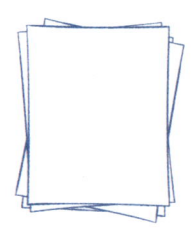
- 10 or more craft sticks 
- Crayons or markers 

LET'S TINKER!

With the help of an adult, **cut out** the rectangles and squares on page 106, the triangles on page 108, and the circles on page 110. **Flip** them, turn them around, and look at their size. Do the shapes remain the same? Now, **close** your eyes, pick up one shape, and feel the edges of the paper. **Count** the number of sides and name the shape.

LET'S MAKE: 2D SHAPE COLLAGE!

1. **Arrange** the shapes you cut out from pages 106, 108, and 110 onto a sheet of paper. (If you need more shapes, **fold**, tear, or cut more out of construction paper with the help of an adult.)

2. Once you have an arrangement you like, **glue** each shape onto the paper.

3. You can **add** materials like ribbon, beads, feathers, or other objects to decorate your collage.

14

2D Shapes

LET'S ENGINEER!

Tinker Town's art museum is opening a gallery called Shape Space! Amelia wants to make some new shape art for the gallery, but she only has craft sticks.

How can Amelia make different shapes using only her craft sticks?

Use your craft sticks to make different shapes on a white piece of paper. How can you combine the craft sticks to make a shape? What shapes can you make? Are there any shapes you can't make with craft sticks? Why or why not? Once you are done arranging your shapes, **glue** them to the paper and decorate your piece of art.

PROJECT 14: DONE!
Get your sticker!

LET'S LEARN ABOUT

Combining 2D Shapes

Draw a line to complete each shape. Then name each shape aloud.

114

15

Combining
2D Shapes

Look at the key, and finish the picture by filling in each shape with the correct color.

COLOR KEY
Square:
Triangle:
Circle:
Rectangle:

Look at the picture. Finish the picture by filling in each shape with the color that matches its features.

COLOR KEY

A shape that has 3 sides: **green**

A shape that has no straight sides: **yellow**

A shape that has 4 sides that are all the same length: **brown**

15

Combining 2D Shapes

Draw a line to match each pair of shapes to their combined shape.

With the help of an adult, cut out the shapes on page 118 and rearrange them into your own forest scene. Then glue them onto this page, and draw any other shapes you may need to finish the scene.

15

Combining 2D Shapes

LET'S START! GATHER THESE TOOLS AND MATERIALS.

| Blocks of different shapes |  Crayons or markers |  Construction paper | 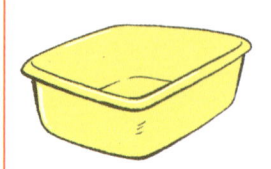 Plastic bin or bucket |
|  Rice, beans, or cornmeal |  Scissors (with an adult's help) |  Glue |  Tape |

LET'S TINKER!

Trace the outline of your blocks onto a piece of construction paper. Then **fill** your bin with rice, beans, or cornmeal. **Bury** your blocks inside so you can't see them anymore. **Reach** into the bin and feel a block. Before pulling it out, **say** what shape it will match on the paper. Then **pull** out the block and put it on the paper to see if you are right. **Continue** matching blocks until there are no more shapes left.

LET'S MAKE: CIRCLE AND SQUARE BIRDS!

1. With the help of an adult, **cut** out a circle and a square from construction paper for the bird bodies.

2. **Glue** these shapes to a piece of white or light-colored construction paper.

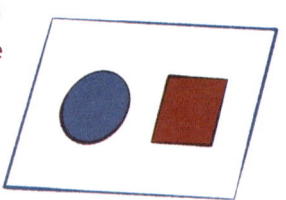

120 TinkerActive Pre-K Math Workbook

3. With the help of an adult, **cut** out 6 small triangles for the beaks and feet. Then **glue** 3 of the triangles to each body.

4. With the help of an adult, **cut** out 2 white circles and 2 smaller black circles for the eyes. **Glue** each white circle onto a body, and each black circle onto a white circle.

5. With the help of an adult, **cut** out 4 half circles for the wings and hair. Then **glue** each set to a body.

6. Display your bird art somewhere special!

15
Combining 2D Shapes

LET'S ENGINEER!

The bees in Bungleburg need a new home—and fast! A bear escaped from the zoo and knocked down all the bees' hives and ate all their honey. The MotMots want to help, but they don't have many materials—just paper and a few tools.

How can the MotMots make a new home for the bees with their materials?

Build the inside of a beehive using paper and your other tools. What shape can you make with paper that looks close to the hive cells that bees climb into? How can you make a lot of those shapes and connect them so many bees can live together?

PROJECT 15: DONE!
Get your sticker!

ANSWER KEY

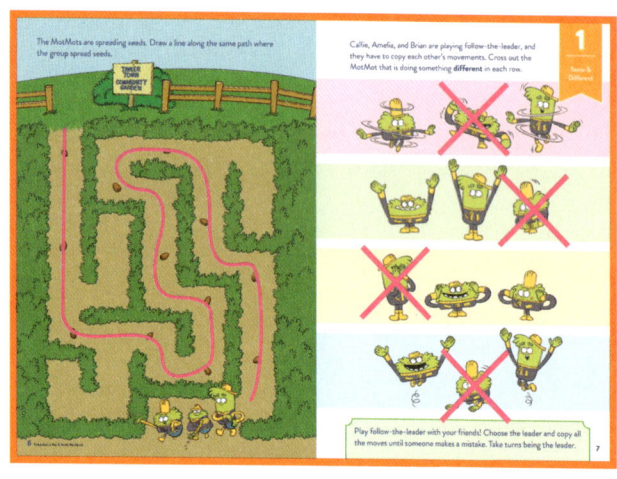

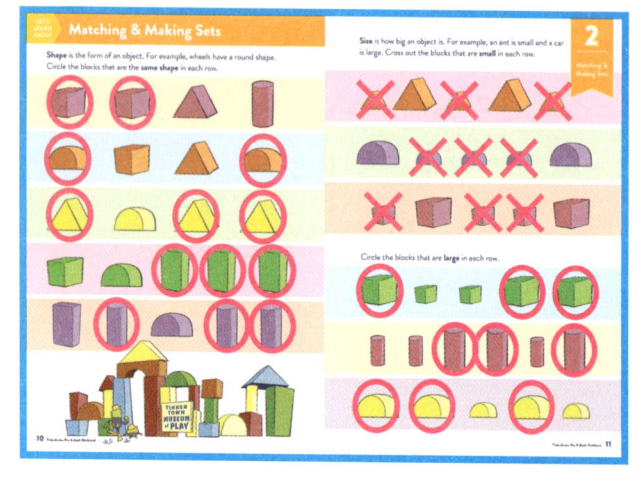

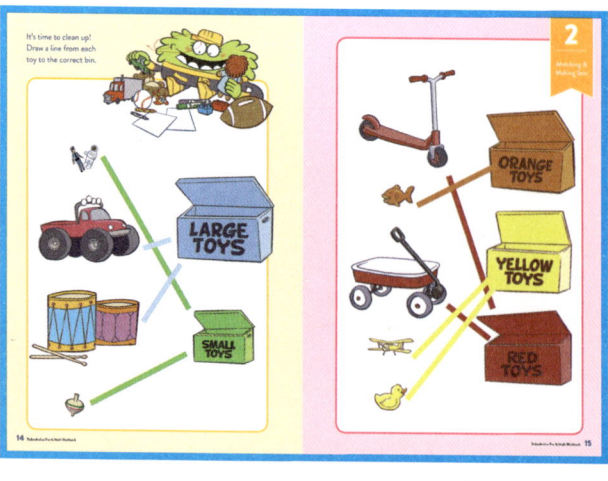

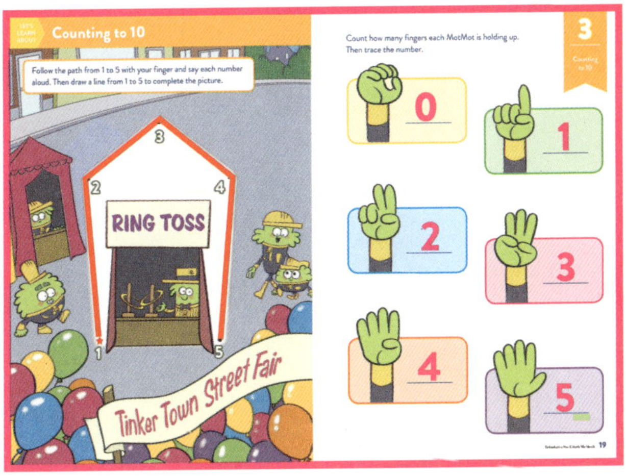

LET'S LEARN ABOUT

Counting to 10

Follow the path from 1 to 5 with your finger and say each number aloud. Then draw a line from 1 to 5 to complete the picture.

Count how many fingers each MotMot is holding up. Then trace the number.

0 1 2 3 4 5

3 Counting to 10

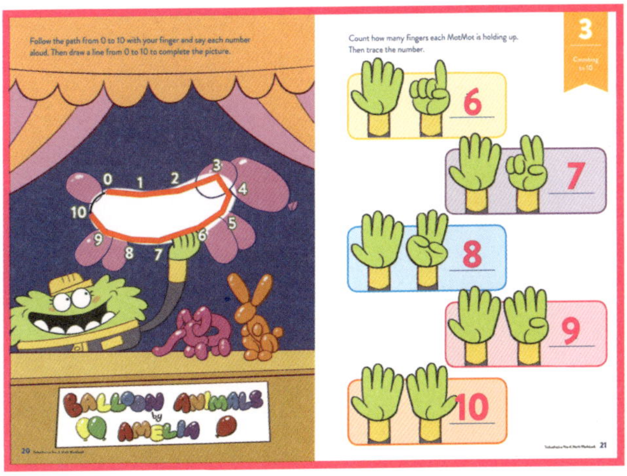

Follow the path from 0 to 10 with your finger and say each number aloud. Then draw a line from 0 to 10 to complete the picture.

Count how many fingers each MotMot is holding up. Then trace the number.

6 7 8 9 10

3 Counting to 10

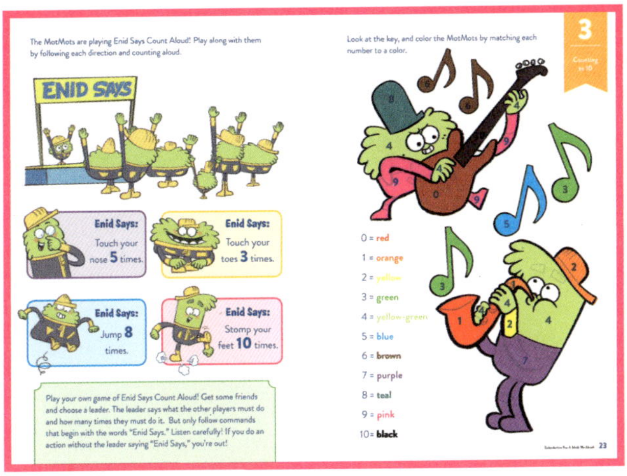

The MotMots are playing Enid Says Count Aloud! Play along with them by following each direction and counting aloud.

Enid Says: Touch your nose **5** times.

Enid Says: Touch your toes **3** times.

Enid Says: Jump **8** times.

Enid Says: Stomp your feet **10** times.

Play your own game of Enid Says Count Aloud! Get some friends and choose a leader. The leader says what the other players must do and how many times they must do it. But only follow commands that begin with the words "Enid Says." Listen carefully! If you do an action without the leader saying "Enid Says," you're out!

Look at the key, and color the MotMots by matching each number to a color.

0 = red
1 = orange
2 = yellow
3 = green
4 = yellow-green
5 = blue
6 = brown
7 = purple
8 = teal
9 = pink
10 = black

3 Counting to 10

LET'S LEARN ABOUT

Quantities 0–5 & Writing 0–5

Count how many pieces of fruit are in each basket. Then write the total number in each basket.

1 2 3 4 5

Hint! You can cross out each piece of fruit as you count so you don't count anything twice.

Count how many of each kind of vegetable are in the basket. Then write the total numbers of each kind of vegetable.

4 5 2 3 1 0

4 Quantities 0–5 & Writing 0–5

Count aloud how many items are in each checkout aisle. The last number you say is the number of objects in the group! Write the total number of items.

2 4 3 5 0

Read the poems aloud to count each group. Then write the number of items in the group.

I count **1** and **2**.
I count 2 stews.

I count **1**, **2**, and **3**.
I count 3 bags of frozen peas.

I count **1**, **2**, **3**, and **4**.
I count 4 pears in the store.

I count 1 cinnamon bun.
Counting food is a lot of fun!

Can you make your own poem for counting to 5?

Answers will vary.

4 Quantities 0–5 & Writing 0–5

With the help of an adult, cut out the items below the baskets. Then sort them into groups. How many of each item do you have? Match the number of items to the correct basket by placing the items on top.

1 2 3 4 5

The MotMots are buying food for a party! Count the number of items each MotMot wants to buy. Then write the number on the cart.

1 2 5 4

4 Quantities 0–5 & Writing 0–5

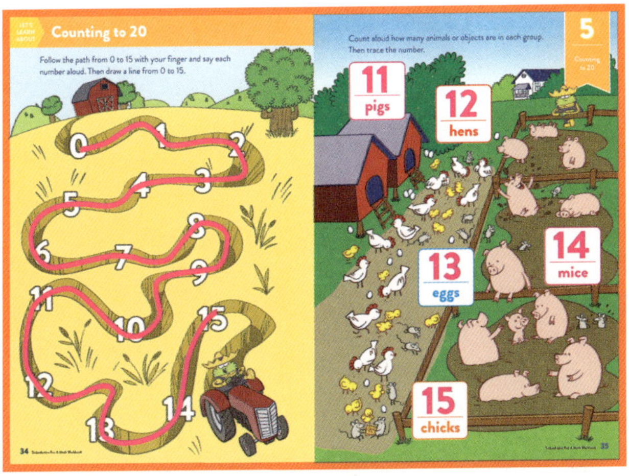

LET'S LEARN ABOUT

Counting to 20

Follow the path from 0 to 15 with your finger and say each number aloud. Then draw a line from 0 to 15.

Count aloud how many animals or objects are in each group. Then trace the number.

11 pigs
12 hens
13 eggs
14 mice
15 chicks

5 Counting to 20

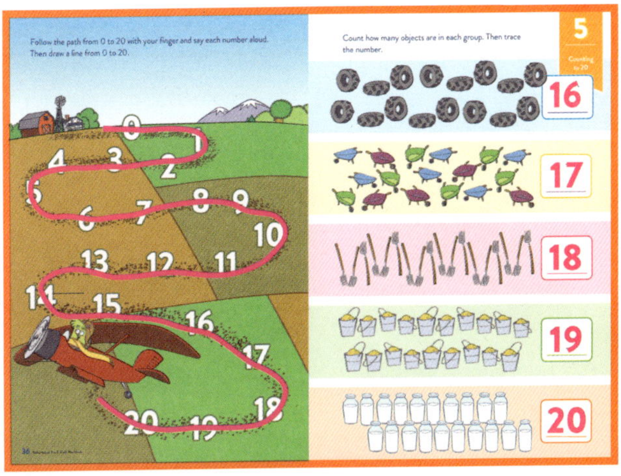

Follow the path from 0 to 20 with your finger and say each number aloud. Then draw a line from 0 to 20.

Count how many objects are in each group. Then trace the number.

16 17 18 19 20

5 Counting to 20

Enid loves eating beans. She loves them so much that she planted 19 different bean plants! Follow the path from 0 to 19 with your finger. Then draw a line from 0 to 19 to connect the bean plants.

If Enid planted 1 more bean plant, how many plants would she have?

Color in the correct number of stalls.

11 8 16 19

Answers will vary.

Answers will vary.

5 Counting to 20

38 39

Quantities to 10 & Writing 6–10

Count how many mountain animals are in each group. Then write the total number of animals in each group. (Hint: You can cross out each animal as you count so you don't count any twice.)

8 hawks
7 yaks
6 cougars
6 woodpeckers
3 owls
5 bears
8 hares
9 tanagers
9 toads
10 chickadees

6 Quantities to 10 & Writing 6–10

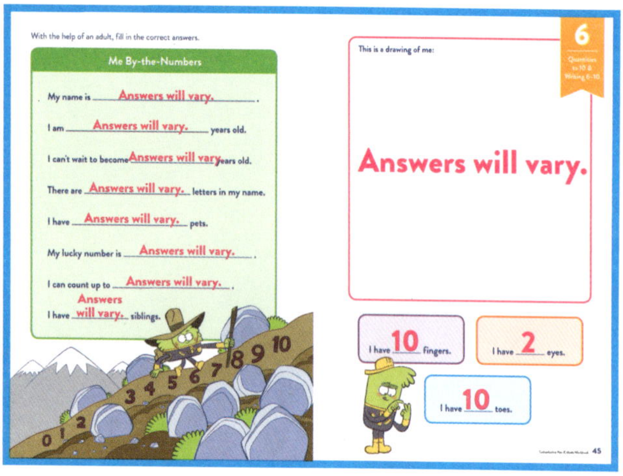
With the help of an adult, fill in the correct answers.

Me By-the-Numbers

My name is Answers will vary.

I am Answers will vary. years old.

I can't wait to become Answers will vary years old.

There are Answers will vary. letters in my name.

I have Answers will vary. pets.

My lucky number is Answers will vary.

I can count up to Answers will vary.

I have Answers will vary. siblings.

This is a drawing of me:

Answers will vary.

I have 10 fingers.

I have 2 eyes.

I have 10 toes.

6 Quantities to 10 & Writing 6–10

45

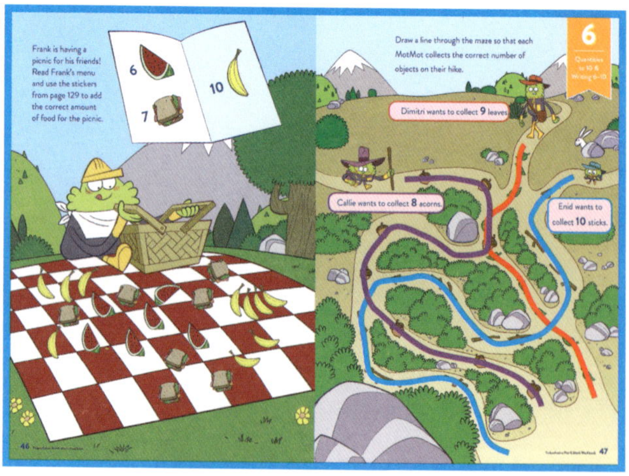
Frank is having a picnic for his friends! Read Frank's menu and use the stickers from page 129 to add the correct amount of food for the picnic.

6 7 10

Draw a line through the maze so that each MotMot collects the correct number of objects on their hike.

Dimitri wants to collect 9 leaves.

Callie wants to collect 8 acorns.

Enid wants to collect 10 sticks.

6 Quantities to 10 & Writing 6–10

46 47

Number Sense

Write the missing numbers on each number line. Then say each number in the line aloud.

1 2 3 4 5
6 7 8 9 10
1 2 3 4 5
6 7 8 9 10

1 2 3 4 5 6 7 8 9 10

7 Number Sense

50 51

Complete the picture by drawing a line from each starting number ★ to 10. Say each number aloud as you go.

Count how many trains are in each group. Then write the number.

3 5 5 2 2

7 Number Sense

52 53

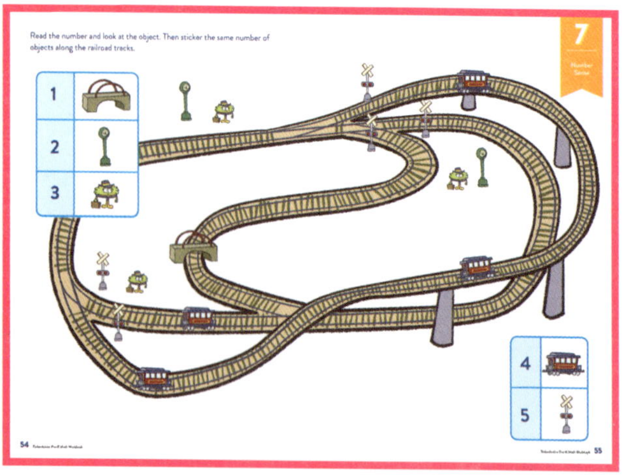
Read the number and look at the object. Then sticker the same number of objects along the railroad tracks.

1	
2	
3	
4	
5	

7 Number Sense

54 55

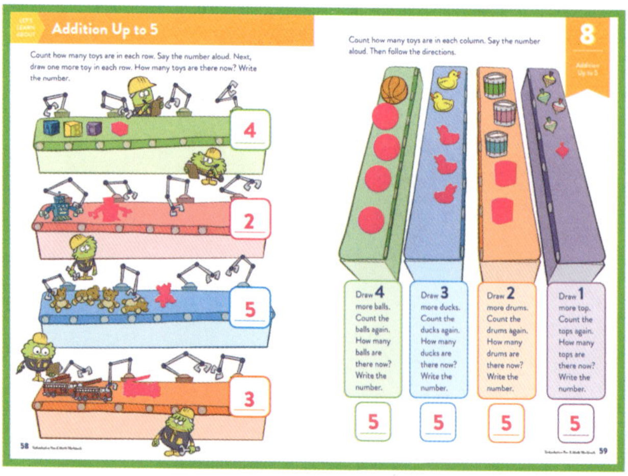
Addition Up to 5

Count how many toys are in each row. Say the number aloud. Next, draw one more toy in each row. How many toys are there now? Write the number.

4 2 5 3

Count how many toys are in each column. Say the number aloud. Then follow the directions.

Draw 4 more balls. Count the balls again. How many balls are there now? Write the number. 5

Draw 3 more ducks. Count the ducks again. How many ducks are there now? Write the number. 5

Draw 2 more drums. Count the drums again. How many drums are there now? Write the number. 5

Draw 1 more top. Count the tops again. How many tops are there now? Write the number. 5

8 Addition Up to 5

58 59

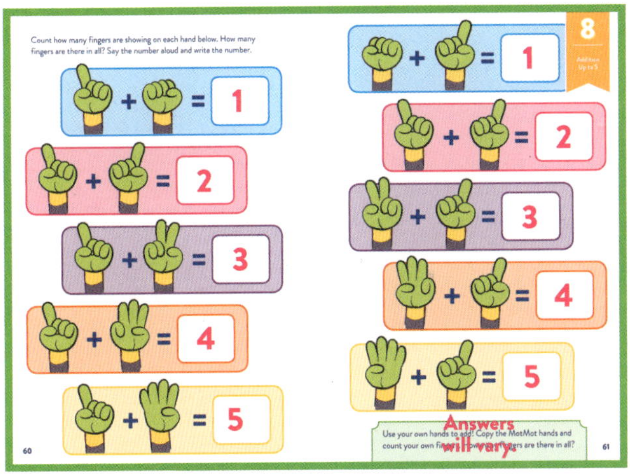
8
Addition Up to 5
Count how many fingers are showing on each hand below. How many fingers are there in all? Say the number aloud and write the number.
1
2
3
4
5
1
2
3
4
5
Answers will vary.
Use your own hands to add! Copy the MotMot hands and count your own fingers. How many fingers are there in all?
60
61

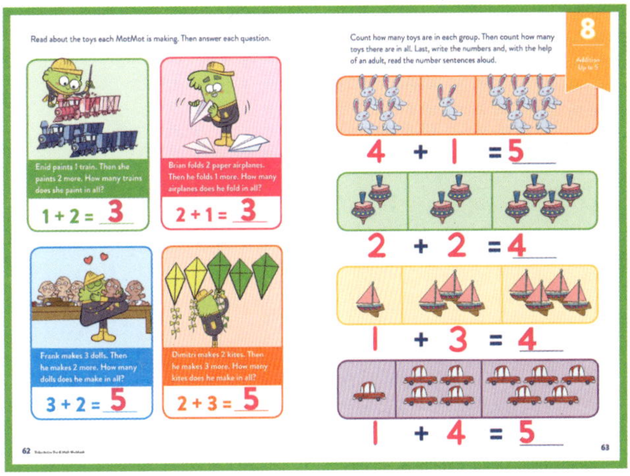
8
Addition Up to 5
Read about the toys each MotMot is making. Then answer each question.
Enid paints 1 train. Then she paints 2 more. How many trains does she paint in all?
1 + 2 = 3
Brian folds 2 paper airplanes. Then he folds 1 more. How many airplanes does he fold in all?
2 + 1 = 3
Frank makes 3 dolls. Then he makes 2 more. How many dolls does he make in all?
3 + 2 = 5
Dimitri makes 2 kites. Then he makes 3 more. How many kites does he make in all?
2 + 3 = 5
Count how many toys are in each group. Then count how many toys there are in all. Last, write the numbers and, with the help of an adult, read the number sentences aloud.
4 + 1 = 5
2 + 2 = 4
1 + 3 = 4
1 + 4 = 5
62
63

Subtraction Under 5
9
Subtraction Under 5
How many balloons does each MotMot have? Count them aloud, then cross out 1 balloon in each group to pop it. How many balloons are left? Count the remaining balloons and write the number.
How many white balloons does each MotMot have? Count them aloud, then color 1 balloon in each group. How many white balloons are left? Write the number.
4
1
2
0
3
2
1
66
67

9
Subtraction Under 5
The MotMots are playing Enid Says Subtract. Read the prompt aloud and use your fingers to subtract. Then write the number.
ENID SAYS SUBTRACT 1 FROM 5.
5 – 1 = 4
ENID SAYS SUBTRACT 2 FROM 5.
5 – 2 = 3
ENID SAYS SUBTRACT 2 FROM 3.
3 – 2 = 1
ENID SAYS SUBTRACT 1 FROM 4.
4 – 1 = 3
ENID SAYS SUBTRACT 4 FROM 5.
5 – 4 = 1
ENID SAYS SUBTRACT 3 FROM 5.
5 – 3 = 2
How many fingers should be up to begin? How many fingers should you put down? The number of fingers that are left up is your answer!
68
69

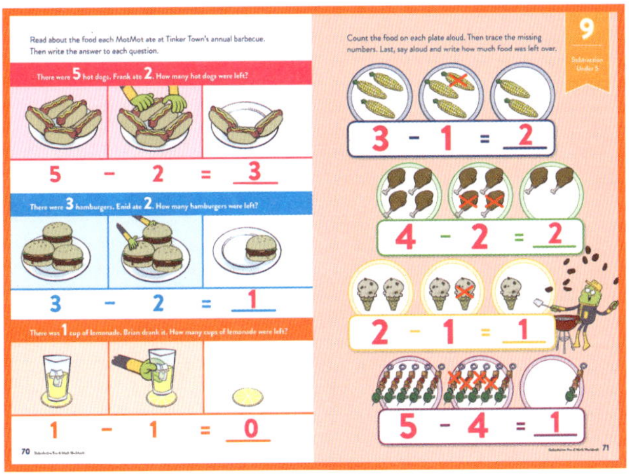
9
Subtraction Under 5
Read about the food each MotMot ate at Tinker Town's annual barbecue. Then write the answer to each question.
There were 5 hot dogs. Frank ate 2. How many hot dogs were left?
5 – 2 = 3
There were 3 hamburgers. Enid ate 2. How many hamburgers were left?
3 – 2 = 1
There was 1 cup of lemonade. Brian drank it. How many cups of lemonade were left?
1 – 1 = 0
Count the food on each plate aloud. Then trace the missing numbers. Last, say aloud and write how much food was left over.
3 – 1 = 2
4 – 2 = 2
2 – 1 = 1
5 – 4 = 1
70
71

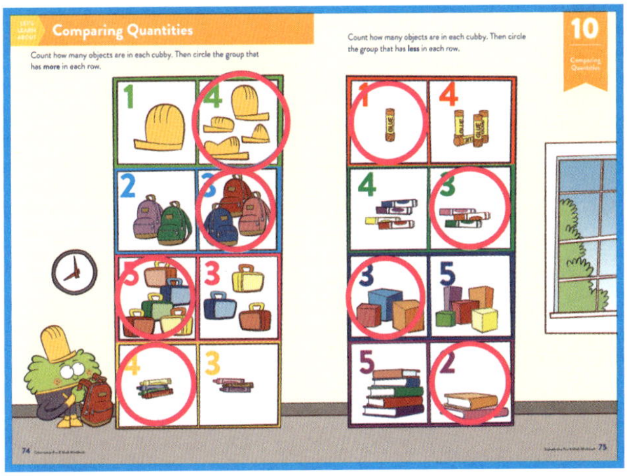
Comparing Quantities
10
Comparing Quantities
Count how many objects are in each cubby. Then circle the group that has more in each row.
1
4
2
3
5
3
4
3
Count how many objects are in each cubby. Then circle the group that has less in each row.
1
4
4
3
3
5
5
2
74
75

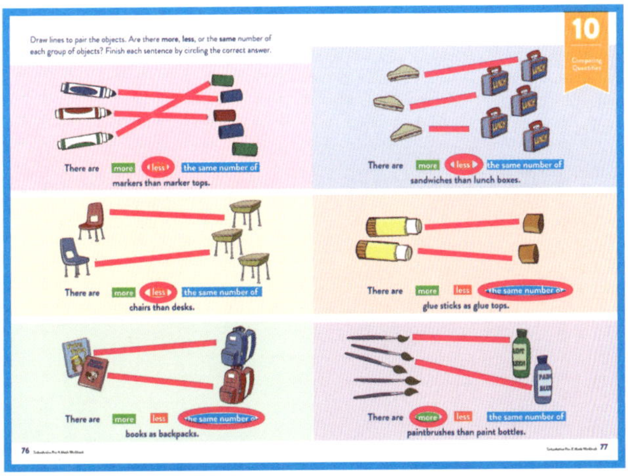
10
Comparing Quantities
Draw lines to pair the objects. Are there more, less, or the same number of each group of objects? Finish each sentence by circling the correct answer.
There are more less the same number of markers than marker tops.
There are more less the same number of sandwiches than lunch boxes.
There are more less the same number of chairs than desks.
There are more less the same number of glue sticks as glue tops.
There are more less the same number of books as backpacks.
There are more less the same number of paintbrushes than paint bottles.
76
77

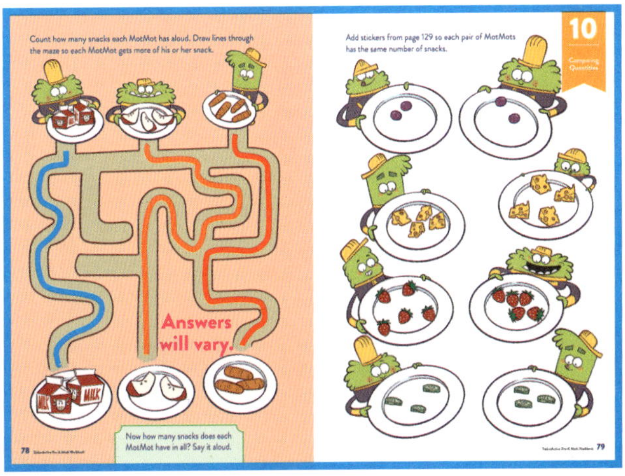
10
Comparing Quantities
Count how many snacks each MotMot has aloud. Draw lines through the maze so each MotMot gets more of his or her snack.
Answers will vary.
Now how many snacks does each MotMot have in all? Say it aloud.
Add stickers from page 129 so each pair of MotMots has the same number of snacks.
78
79

Measurement
Circle the object that is bigger in each row. Then underline the object that is smaller.
Circle the object that is taller in each scene. Then underline the object that is shorter.
11
82
83

Circle the object that is longer in each row. Then underline the object that is shorter.
SKEE BALL
SKEE BALL
Circle the object that is heavier in each box. Then underline the object that is lighter.
11
84
85

Circle the tallest MotMot in each row. Underline the shortest MotMot in each row.
AMELIA
BRIAN
FRANK
DIMITRI
ENID
CALLIE
With the help of an adult, cut out the MotMots on page 86. Then place each MotMot next to the ride entrance. Which MotMots can ride on the roller coaster? Say their names aloud.
11
You must be THIS TALL to ride
Brian
Dimitri
86
87

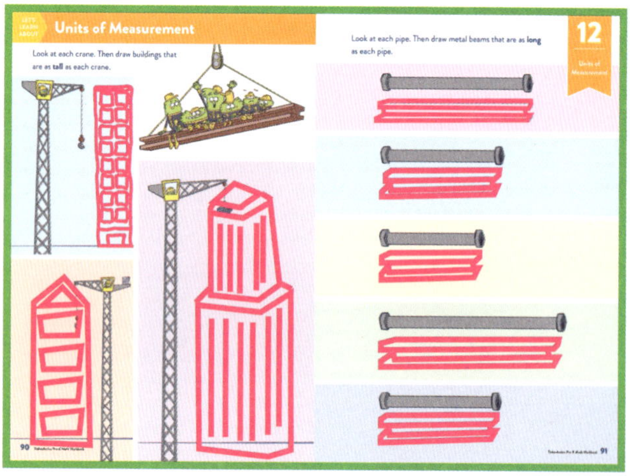
Units of Measurement
Look at each crane. Then draw buildings that are as tall as each crane.
Look at each pipe. Then draw metal beams that are as long as each pipe.
12
90
91

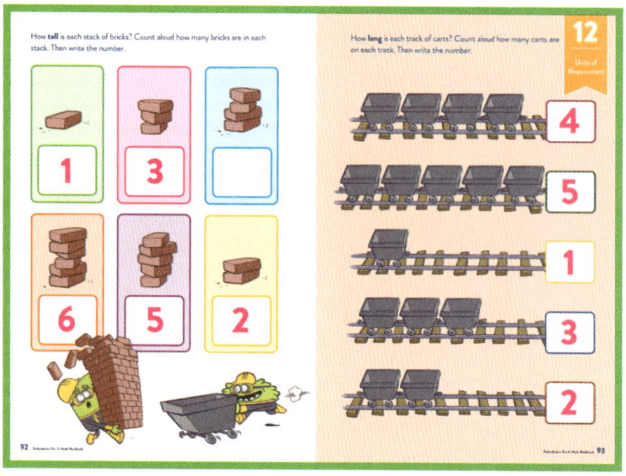
How tall is each stack of bricks? Count aloud how many bricks are in each stack. Then write the number.
1
3
6
5
2
How long is each track of carts? Count aloud how many carts are on each track. Then write the number.
12
4
5
1
3
2
92
93

How many bricks tall is each object? Count how many bricks are beside each object. Then write the number.
STOP
3
2
1
5
4
How many bricks long is each object? Count how many bricks are underneath each object. Then write the number.
12
4
1
2
3
5
94
95

Spatial Reasoning
Color the books on the top shelf red. Then color the books on the bottom shelf blue.
TINKER TOWN LIBRARY
READ!
Circle the MotMots that are in front of the bookshelves. Underline the MotMots that are next to the bookshelves.
13
Find the MotMots that are behind the bookshelves. How many are there? Say the number aloud.
98
99

Circle the MotMots that are walking up the stairs. Underline the MotMots that are walking down the stairs.
MATH BOOKS
SCIENCE BOOKS
HISTORY BOOKS
PICTURE BOOKS
Get the MotMot stickers from page 129. Place the MotMots on the carpet for story time!
13
Find the MotMots in the reading nooks. How many are there? Say the number aloud.
100
101

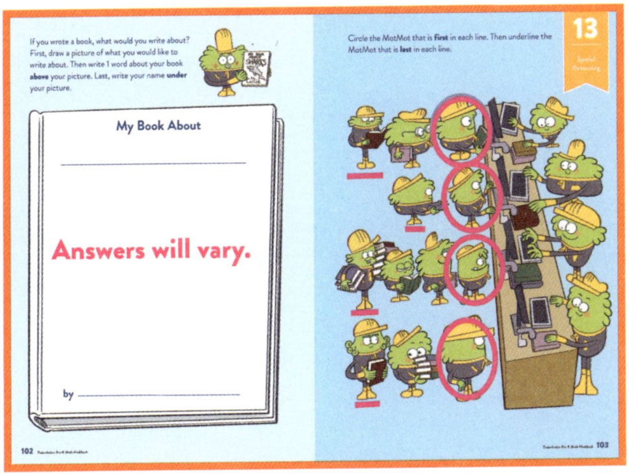

13

Spatial Reasoning

If you wrote a book, what would you write about? First, draw a picture of what you would like to write about. Then write 1 word about your book **above** your picture. Last, write your name **under** your picture.

My Book About

by

Answers will vary.

Circle the MotMot that is **first** in each line. Then underline the MotMot that is **last** in each line.

102 103

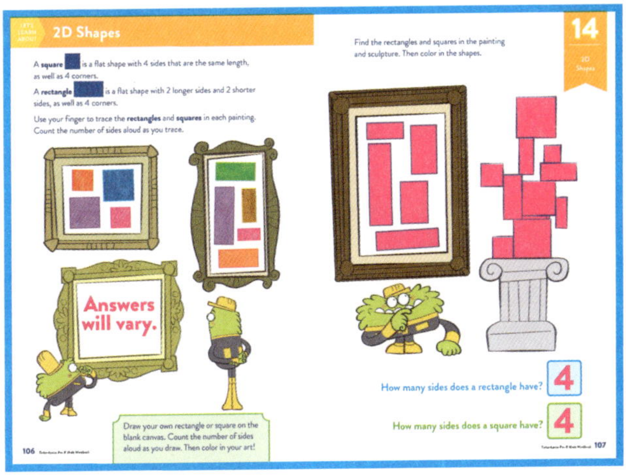

2D Shapes

14

2D Shapes

A **square** is a flat shape with 4 sides that are the same length, as well as 4 corners.

A **rectangle** is a flat shape with 2 longer sides and 2 shorter sides, as well as 4 corners.

Use your finger to trace the **rectangles** and **squares** in each painting. Count the number of sides aloud as you trace.

Answers will vary.

Draw your own rectangle or square on the blank canvas. Count the number of sides aloud as you draw. Then color in your art!

Find the rectangles and squares in the painting and sculpture. Then color in the shapes.

How many sides does a rectangle have? 4

How many sides does a square have? 4

106 107

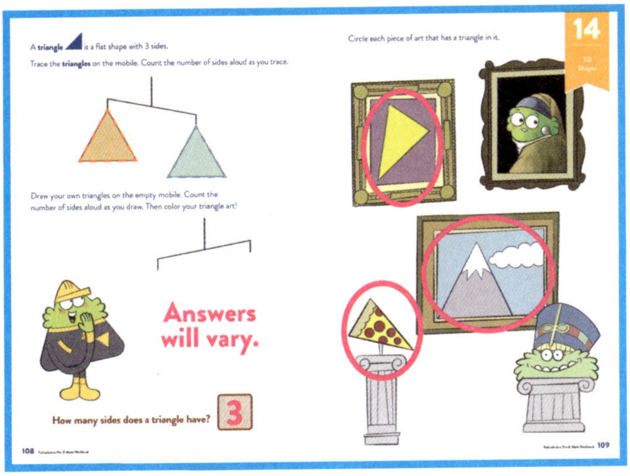

14

2D Shapes

A **triangle** is a flat shape with 3 sides.

Trace the **triangles** on the mobile. Count the number of sides aloud as you trace.

Draw your own triangles on the empty mobile. Count the number of sides aloud as you draw. Then color your triangle art!

Answers will vary.

How many sides does a triangle have? 3

Circle each piece of art that has a triangle in it.

108 109

14

2D Shapes

A **circle** is a flat shape made by a curved line. It has no sides.

Trace each **circle**. Describe the shape aloud as you trace.

How many sides does a circle have? 0

Draw and color your own circle on the empty pedestal!

Draw lines to match the objects to their shapes. Then say the shapes aloud.

ADMIT ONE

I ♥ ART

circle

rectangle

triangle

Find objects around you that are shaped like rectangles, squares, circles, and triangles. Then draw them below.

Answers will vary.

110 111

Combining 2D Shapes

15

Combining 2D Shapes

Draw a line to complete each shape. Then name each shape aloud.

TINKER TOWN NATURE PATH

15

Combining 2D Shapes

Look at the key, and finish the picture by filling in each shape with the correct color.

COLOR KEY

Square:

Triangle:

Circle:

Rectangle:

Look at the key. Finish the picture by filling in each shape with the color that matches its features.

COLOR KEY

A shape that has 3 sides: green

A shape that has no straight sides: yellow

A shape that has 4 sides that are all the same length: brown

15

Combining 2D Shapes

Draw a line to match each pair of shapes to their combined shape.

With the help of an adult, cut out the shapes on page 118 and rearrange them into your own forest scene. Then glue them onto this page, and draw any other shapes you may need to finish the scene.

Answers will vary.

118

Odd Dot
120 Broadway
New York, NY 10271
OddDot.com

Copyright © 2020 by Odd Dot

By purchasing this workbook, the buyer is permitted to reproduce pages for classroom use only, but not for commercial resale. Please contact the publisher for permission to reproduce pages for an entire school or school district. With the exception of the above, no portion of this book may be reproduced—mechanically, electronically, or by any other means, including photocopying—without written permission of the publisher.

ISBN: 978-1-250-20809-5

WRITER   Nathalie Le Du
ILLUSTRATOR   Les McClaine
EDUCATIONAL CONSULTANT   Randi House
CHARACTER DESIGNER   Anna-Maria Jung
COVER ILLUSTRATOR   Anna-Maria Jung
LEAD SERIES DESIGNER   Carolyn Bahar
INTERIOR DESIGNERS   Colleen AF Venable and Phil Conigliaro
COVER DESIGNER   Tae Won Yu
EDITOR   Kate Avino

Our books may be purchased in bulk for promotional, educational, or business use. Please contact your local bookseller or the Macmillan Corporate and Premium Sales Department at (800) 221-7945 ext. 5442 or by email at MacmillanSpecialMarkets@macmillan.com.

DISCLAIMER
The publisher and authors disclaim responsibility for any loss, injury, or damages caused as a result of any of the instructions described in this book.

TinkerActive is a trademark of Odd Dot.
Printed in China by Hung Hing Off-set Printing Co. Ltd., Heshan City, Guangdong Province
First edition, 2020

10 9 8 7 6 5 4 3 2 1